Incredible LIFE MAKEOVER

Step-by-Step Transformation to Wholeness

Endorsements

Vibrantly written and chock-full of nuggets of wisdom, *Incredible Life Makeover* helps you find your way out of a painful life situation. Julie's insightful and interactive approach provides you with step-by-step helps that guide you like a roadmap. Fresh and inspiring—you'll find yourself dog-earing the pages for future reference! It will become a book you'll want to gift to someone you love. Enjoy!

—**Mark Hendrickson,**
Dwelling Place Ministries
Author of *Supernatural Provision*, Kansas City, MO

Julie gives profound analogies and articulate prayers by expounding on the truth Jesus spoke of in the Lord's Prayer along with examples of the healthy thoughts and actions of a person who is free from the curse of an unforgiving heart. She rightly identifies forgiveness as an act of our will and a process through which we gain peace and true joy in our lives. I wholeheartedly endorse *Incredible Life Makeover.*

—**Sara Renner, Songwriter & Recording Artist**
Co-composer of Song "Forgive," Minneapolis, MN

What you hold in your hands is more than a book. You are holding Julie's life. It has been said the best books are a revelation of the who the author is, their truest self, and more like holding a human in written form . . . well, this written labor is exactly that! Julie has risked being completely vulnerable with her readers in order to call them into their destiny and healing. Every author lives with the pleasure and terror of being "real" and thus, making their written projects something more like their baby than simply a binding of pages. I wholeheartedly recommend *Incredible Life Makeover* to the hurting and the hungry. Prepare for YOUR life to experience a supernatural makeover!

—**Pastor Randy Dean**
Living Word Chapel,
Author of *Radiance*, Glenwood City, WI

I thought freedom from drugs and alcohol would change me into the complete person I had never been previously. But my identity as a "sober person" felt incomplete and often left me emotionally exhausted. *Incredible Life Makeover* showed me how to take control of my thoughts and emotions instead of letting them control me. I have learned a new level of freedom by rejecting fear, putting my emotions in the caboose, and learning to see myself as God sees me, instead of being concerned about how others see me. I have discovered my true identity!

—**Heather C.**
Eau Claire, WI

I have watched Julie's transformation over two decades as she grew through the storms of life as described in the *Incredible Life Makeover*. Her wisdom and biblical strategies provide a rock solid plan to be prayerfully worked through one concept at a time. God wants the same freedom for you that Julie has experienced. Are you ready for your incredible life makeover?

—Lynn Dehnke
Author of *Meditate and Declare*, Eau Claire, WI

It has been a great pleasure to partner with Julie, in Kenya and in the United States, to share the good news of God's love and grace and to rescue people from life's distressing situations. I have been moved by her passion to see lives changed, healed and restored.

Her gift of teaching reaches children and adults. My wife and I are so happy to know her and call her friend.

—**Bishop Francis Macharia**
House of Hope, Nairobi, Kenya

Do you need a restart? Wherever you are at with your walk with God, Julie encourages and leads you step-by-step into a closer relationship with Him. *Incredible Life Makeover* benefits women and men; it is for teenagers and adults of any age. I grew so much through applying her advice. When you complete one phase of transformation, read the book again to gain more knowledge and new skills to complete the next phase.

—**Andrea L.**,
Chippewa Falls, WI

Incredible LIFE MAKEOVER

Step-by-Step Transformation to Wholeness

JULIE COURT

REDEMPTION PRESS

Published by Redemption Press, PO Box 427, Enumclaw, WA 98022 Toll Free (844) 2REDEEM (273-3336).

Redemption Press is honored to present this title in partnership with the author. The views expressed or implied in this work are those of the author. Redemption Press provides our imprint seal representing design excellence, creative content and high quality production.

ISBN 13: 978-1-63232-761-1 (Print)
         978-1-63232-762-8 (ePub)
         978-1-63232-764-2 (Mobi)

Library of Congress Catalog Card Number: 2015950658

CONTENTS

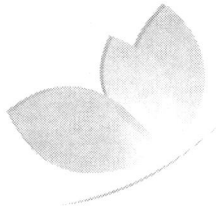

Part II
Living in Freedom

PREFACE

I would like to dedicate this book to my three children, their spouses, and my granddaughter, Jaiden. It has been my privilege and great delight to be a mother and grandmother. I am so proud to see you building your lives and families. Spending time with all of you is my greatest joy. As I watch you mature, I can't help but reflect on our journey and how much you have taught me. I love you and look forward to building a legacy together.

In order to help as many people as possible, I have shared tender details about what happened during my childhood. I am thankful our family has overcome our painful past, shared many wonderful times, and continues to celebrate milestones together. I would like to express my gratitude to my mom, dad and his wife, sister and her family, and my brother and his family; you have all blessed me beyond words by your faithful commitment to family.

I hope *Incredible Life Makeover* clearly and concisely communicates the knowledge I have gained during my life transitions to aid in the recovery of those who are hurting.

Bringing this book to life took the help and support of many people. I would like to thank my editor, Monica Miller, for her technical expertise, spiritual input, and overall guidance. I am especially appreciative of the time spent reviewing the manuscript for content and readability by my friends: Chris, Heather, Cheryl, and Lynn. I also wish to convey my gratitude to my graphic designer, Leila Wilson, for designing the book cover, which is a work of art. I would also like to acknowledge my contacts at the Western Wisconsin Christian Writer's Guild, whose efforts helped me sharpen my writing skills.

My life has been enriched by the teaching of God's Word through multiple churches and ministries. A special thank you to my extended family of fellow believers in my home church in Eau Claire, WI; I could not have completed this project without you. Thank you for continuing to believe in me during my ultimate test and holding me accountable to my calling and destiny. I am grateful for the love and kindness of so many friends: Andrea, Bonnie, Jenni, Katie, Robin, Tracy, Kelli, Brenda, Sue, Kari, Rusty, Karen and everyone else too numerous to mention.

Regardless of why or what caused our particular situation, when we need to begin again, we can put the puzzle pieces back together with God's help. Through a step-by-step transformation, we can enjoy living in freedom.

I hope you enjoy the *Incredible Life Makeover*. May it speed you along in your journey toward healing and wholeness.

PART I
SEVEN PHASES OF TRANSFORMATION

THE DOOR TO TRANSFORMATION

" I *just want to be normal. Why can't I be happy like everyone else?"* rolled around in my thirteen-year-old head as the TV droned on. The smiling faces mocked me. Slinking further into the drab green fabric of the couch, I tried to drown out desperate thoughts about what would happen if he found us again. My child-like hope clashed against my gnawing fear. As the hours dragged by, anxiety clawed at my insides. Frantic thoughts consumed me. *"Is this all I have to look forward to? It can't be; I'm barely surviving."*

Hope died as I heard a fist punch the door. My stepfather's voice pierced the darkness. "I know you are in there. Open the door!" With despair closing in around me, my childhood dream of being anything I wanted was sucked into a murky abyss. I trembled as fear reigned; panic rampaged my thoughts. *Oh no! He found us. Not again. I can't breathe.* More banging filled the air. *Please God, not again.* My nightmare was to be repeated as we opened the door and horror stepped in.

The *Incredible Life Makeover* tells the story of how God takes broken lives and makes them whole. Many years ago, I was that young girl. It was a terrible day during a disturbing period of my life. But with God's help, I eventually experienced my first transformation. As a result of other distressing transitions sprinkled throughout my journey, I have been through a few more makeovers. Being guided by the Holy Spirit, I came out victorious.

God's ways surpassed all of my plans.[1] Doing life His way brought His protection, provision, and promotion into my life. While I have known pain, loss and heartache, I am happy and enjoying my journey.

If you or a loved one are being crushed by a painful life situation, the *Incredible Life Makeover* is a roadmap to help you rebuild one or more areas of your life. Even if it doesn't look like it right now, God loves you and has a great plan for your life. The seven phases described in the *Incredible Life Makeover* can help you move from brokenness to wholeness. You may find the biblical strategies in one of the phases are just what you are looking for. For those in a more serious situation, you may need to work through all seven. If I can do it after having my life touched by alcoholism, mental abuse, codependence, career changes, unemployment, the threat of bankruptcy and divorce, you can too!

What will our lives look like after our makeover is complete? We will:

- Wake in the morning knowing we are deeply loved and valued
- Trade the spirit of heaviness for hope and healing
- Face the day's opportunities and struggles with relentless courage
- Make decisions based on time-tested eternal principles
- Enjoy living with vision to fulfill our purpose

Too many people choose to go through life miserable, drugged up, and comfortably numb. They plod mechanically along like robots, enduring each day. Countless people suffer with debilitating depression. Thoughts of, *No one cares. Go ahead and do it. Kill yourself,* pummel them. The afflicted spend hours running from demeaning thoughts of, *You are worthless and always will be.* The hurting cringe as they hear taunting accusations like, *Failure! You are just like your father!* After hearing these vile voices, the torment drives the afflicted to unleash harm on themselves or others.

When will it stop? The rivers of soul-wrenching pain stop when the right actions are taken to silence the voices.

Do you (or does someone close to you) escape from the intense pressure and pace of life with excessive food, alcohol, or drugs? Do you evade reality by continually watching television, playing video games, shopping excessively, or using addictive substances? Do you wander from one relationship to the next? Do you wish you knew how to change? Are you looking for help?

I can relate.

Before finding the courage to change, my own anger, soul pain, and bitterness hung over my life like a burial garment. The decay oozed out onto everything I touched. No matter how hard I tried, I couldn't ignore the negativity I carried. My attempts to break free were futile until I finally found the source of true goodness, which empowered me to break out of my cycle of destruction. Here is a peek into my story and how I discovered the doorway to transformation.

The Dark Days

The drums of divorce beat over and over in my ten-year-old mind. *I can't believe it. It must be my fault my parents are splitting up. If only I had behaved, maybe this wouldn't be happening.*

After my mother announced, "Your father is leaving," the back steps of our farmhouse became my personal courtroom. I jumped back and forth from self-condemnation to self-pity and back again.

I didn't understand how this could have happened. I had experienced many uplifting, joyful times with my parents, along with the downs that came with weekends of heavy drinking and family time couched in codependence. As a child growing up, my parents had dropped me off at church because I wanted to hear more about God. Even though I could sense the tension in our home, I never expected the *D* word.

Like Humpty Dumpty, I was not sure anyone could put my life back together again. I felt lost and unwanted as my father moved out and began binge drinking.

My existence descended from miserable to wretched when my mother married an abuser on the rebound. Our knight in shining armor proved to be physically and mentally abusive. After finding his personal stash of pornography, I was even more revolted by him. Feeling trapped in the abusive terror, I began to withdraw and prayed for deliverance.

One night my mother secretly fled with my siblings and me and tried to hide. Over and over I prayed under my breath, "God, please don't let him find us!" I despaired when he tracked us down and dragged us back. Regardless of my heart's cry, we left and returned back to the torture many times. Each time the trauma resumed, my trust in God withered a little more, until I didn't believe He cared at all. I thought, *If He lets this happen over and over, what kind of God is He?*

One day during a car ride, my stepfather ran his hand along the top of the seat and rested it suggestively on my shoulder. My stomach turned because of some of the things I knew but never uttered. I turned in disgust and warned him, "If you ever touch me, I'll slit your throat." Previously I had found one of his hunting knives in the bedroom; I meant every word. Hatred festered in my heart.

One night the situation degraded into him terrorizing my mother with a gun and firing a shot through the ceiling. I watched her faint and fall to the floor. My mother was transported by ambulance to the hospital while having a nervous breakdown. As I witnessed the trauma, I lost all hope.

Instinctively, I knew I had to save myself. As my mother lay in a hospital bed, I issued an ultimatum, "Let me go live with Grandma and Grandpa, or I will become a prostitute! I am not living one more day with that maniac!"

These were the words of a desperate teenager expecting to be on the run. I couldn't stay to protect her. I left with my grandparents—severely damaged, but alive.

Throughout the next year, I hid in the comfort of my grandparents' stable home, ate rice pudding, and slid safely into bed. Their gentle love covered my woundedness. The soothing atmosphere eased my emotional trauma and calmed my terror so I could sleep.

I feared a loveless future. I didn't think anyone would ever want me so I focused on excelling in high school to prepare for a lucrative career in computers. I mistakenly thought if I was totally self-sufficient, I could keep other people from disappointing me.

I felt rejected and insecure. I maneuvered through school days with a protective cloak, petrified to let anyone in. I didn't want anyone to know what I had lived through. I needed to hide myself; I needed to hide my shame.

Little did I know, a needed course correction was approaching on the horizon. My safe but dark prison would eventually give way through exposure to a powerful alluring light.

An Alluring Light

Miriam entered my life quite by accident. Her friendship changed my life. We frequently sat in the hallway after lunch discussing life, God, and Friday night plans. She listened with compassion as I raged against God and demanded answers to impossible questions like, "If God is love, why do babies die?" She rode home on the bus, researched my questions, discussed them with her mother, and came back with answers I had never heard before. I wondered if Miriam's God was real.

My anger over the unanswered prayers and the pain of my haunted past continued to spill out. I grilled her with, "If God loves me so much, why did He let all this happen to me?" She tried to explain how men and women had been given a free will because they were created in God's image. The choices of adults in my life had caused what had happened. She went on to explain why God wouldn't step in and take back control. Man's free will was given to empower us to sow good things or bad things into our lives and the lives around us. More research, answers, and persistent love continued to flow in my direction.

Miriam tried to tell me about Jesus. I could not comprehend the depth of His love for me. How could I be so precious to Jesus that He would suffer to pay for my freedom? As He faced the cross, Jesus had looked at me through time and chose to love and place a high value on me, even when I hated Him because of what I had gone through. Deep inside, I didn't understand His unconditional love. Why would God even want me after what I had been through? My shame and erroneous need to earn God's approval blocked my vision.

Miriam invited me home to the farm; I met her parents, her brothers, and her younger sister. After the barn chores were done, we warmed our hands and cold feet by the wood stove; its heat radiated from the living room to the rest of the house. With ice on the inside of the windows, we slept upstairs and talked under the quilts on cold January nights. Although there were plenty of interesting things to do outside, I preferred being in the kitchen as her mother, Ellen, made supper. Although strange to me, reading God's Word and praying were normal here.

I observed a loving family, committed to each other, but far from perfect. I was touched by a sweetness that drew me like metal to a magnet.

Soon, another friend had me over for dinners and teenage activities. Her parents reached out to share their knowledge of God's Word with me. My connections to other teens expanded.

Love came knocking on my door, demanding an audience with my mind, will, and emotions. During overnights, skating parties, and youth events, my friends met my deepest need for acceptance. Over family dinners, their parents dispensed comforting wisdom to combat my bitterness against those in authority, and especially against God. As they gave me rides and offered a listening ear, my friends' families expressed the unfailing kindness of God. Their unconditional love slowly, silently dissolved its way through my tough outer defenses. Like the slow drip of water on a sand castle, my walls began to crumble.

I was so programmed by dysfunction it was hard to imagine a peaceful, stable future. My deep-seated resentment and anger were poisonous. I mistakenly thought if I didn't expect anything good, I would not be disappointed. But the overcoming power of love dug small openings for hope and healing to leak in.

*Unconditional love became a reality to me through ordinary people expressing and explaining an **extraordinary** God.*

Never-changing truth, combined with actions based on real, tangible love I could feel and touch from ordinary people, slowly peeled away the layers.

One day a single ray of unconditional love finally penetrated; hope was birthed inside my stony heart. This hope was a life-giving, life-changing, powerful force. The reality of what God's character looked like, and what His nature felt like, began to permeate my thoughts. As I read more of the Bible, I began to picture God differently.

My heart screamed for love and freedom. I became conflicted and at odds with myself. Why continue to reject what I desperately craved? Fear and love could not both rule my heart: perfect love casts out fear.[2] Did I have the courage to change? Could I trust God again? Should I risk leaving my safe prison to step out into the light and embrace freedom? I considered placing my broken life into the hands of a living, loving God.

Saying "Yes"

One weekend I found myself at a youth group conference in Green Lake, Wisconsin. Around midnight, I finally yielded to this unrestricted, unreserved love that was pursuing and wooing me no matter what I said or did. I tearfully surrendered my bloody wounds, deafening fears, and painful failures into God's hands. Sitting side by side in the empty stairwell, Ellen put her arm around me and led in a simple prayer:

Dear Jesus, I want you in my life. I know I have done things and said things that were wrong. Would you please forgive me? I accept you, Jesus, as my Savior. Thank you for paying the price for my sins. I am broken and need you to be Lord over my life. I surrender to you. I receive your love and forgiveness. I am a new creation. I am yours. In Jesus' name, Amen.

I surrendered my life permanently into the hands of Jesus. For the first time in years, I felt connected to God as I was immersed in His unconditional love. I believed God's love had the power to heal the wounds destruction had sown in my life. Joy flooded my soul and illuminated my thoughts. My heart felt so light all of a sudden. Tears of relief streamed down my face as I felt the encompassing love of God hugging me. His voice whispered, "I love you, Julie. I love you."

He whispers to all His children. He loves to whisper your name.

I felt such freedom from the terrible burden I had carried. My heart was full of a peace I couldn't fully understand. I felt so alive! I could not contain my joy. The adventure of becoming whole and learning how to live differently was about to begin. Hope and courage were planted in my heart. I wanted to dream again. I wanted to really live.

Coming Alive

Imagine coming home to find an exquisite, expensive birthday present on the kitchen table, wrapped in foil gift wrap with an extravagant-looking red bow. The priceless gift of rescue awaits, ready to be accepted and unwrapped, because Jesus paid the ultimate price for our sin. When we are finally ready to admit our way isn't working out so well, we say yes to an unbelievable gift that lasts for a lifetime. Through an act of faith, we put our lives into the loving, protective hands of God. We find recreation, reconciliation, and restoration.

Life has joy and sorrow mixed together. Our life stories are unique. As individuals, we decide how to handle the situations we face. Will we go it alone or ask God to walk beside us in our journey? Because God is a gentleman, he waits for an invitation to come in to our heart.

One of the most exciting faith stories I have ever heard was from a friend of mine named Suzie. Although she was married, Suzie was a drug-addicted stripper whose life was off track. She loved the rebellion and reveling in the attention of men. She didn't have a trustworthy compass to steer her life. She describes that phase of her life as being in a pigpen, getting dirtier and dirtier. After finding a relationship with Christ, now she treasures her husband, enjoys being married, and considers it a high priority to be a godly mother for her two young children. Jesus gave her a makeover! She now reaches out to women in crisis with love, hope, and truth.

Jesus brings guidance and contentment in daily living. I have another friend, Miranda, whose dad left when she was six years old and never came back. Although she was beautiful on the outside, she struggled with feeling unwanted and abandoned. Even though she was married, she was unhappy. Inner pain lured her into looking to another married man for comfort and companionship. Tragedy struck. It took years to undo the damage, but God gave her a makeover. She is thriving and walking in freedom today.

If you are hunting for answers as solid as a rock, keep reading. Pushing past the discomfort of self-exposure, I offer you the insights and effective tools I gained while pressing toward wholeness. These powerful principles have stood the test over time; when they are put into action, these life skills help anyone build a life filled with purpose, and rich, meaningful relationships. A clear picture of the transformation process will unfold as I share more of my thoughts and experiences and interesting stories about people from all walks of life.

The power in God's love gives us the strength to hold on when we are beyond our natural capacity to keep going. God's love changes us from the inside out one day at a time.

His love becomes our source of patience in adversity and kindness in times of criticism. Supernatural love gives us the vision to believe for the best when the evidence of the past tells us to do otherwise. In the fight against overwhelming evils, God's love helps us to rejoice when truth and justice prevail. God's love believes all things, hopes all things, and endures all things; God's love still stands when all else has fallen.[3] His love truly is the overriding power on Earth!

Letting God love you and saying yes to His leading is the doorway to your incredible life makeover. You are valuable; let's get started on your exciting journey!

A CLEAN HEART

The second phase of transformation is learning to walk in forgiveness. We overcome our past by forgiving those who have hurt us. It is easier to drop the backpack of guilt and shame if we also learn to forgive ourselves for our mistakes, however tragic. Learning to forgive can determine our level of freedom and future success. Unforgiveness casts a shadow over a life; forgiveness illuminates it.

Forgiveness is a supernatural force in our lives. Whether or not we are walking as one of God's children, when we choose to forgive, we receive a blessing. It is a law in the universe. Through the supernatural power of forgiveness, we can learn to walk above the forces trying to bring us down. Meditate on these for inspiration:

- The greater the pain, the greater the final blessing after forgiving your abuser.
- The greater the insult, the greater the relief when we forgive and lighten our load.

- The greater the injury, the greater the need to forgive and walk toward healing.

≈

As I emerged from the darkest period of my life, Christ filled my deepest needs for unconditional love and acceptance; I lived with a new purpose. At first I couldn't believe I was treasured by the Designer of the universe, my Creator. I felt His approval as His Spirit became my constant companion. As I biked through the streets of my city, unbroken songs of praise bubbled from my lips. This was a radical change from my past endless wandering to avoid going home to a depressing reality.

My newly-found faith sprouted transformation in my inner being.

After asking Christ to be my Savior and Lord, my life began to be refashioned by the Father's touch. Jesus occupied my heart, but my past was still outwardly demonstrated in my habits, hungers, and hobbies. Though I was overwhelmed by my emotional issues, I counted on God to change me. One by one, God gently uncovered the root causes for my destructive mindsets, habits, and responses. With the Holy Spirit as my Helper, I worked on replacing each of them with a new, positive one.

Even though I was unsure of what to say or how to act, I overflowed with passion for God, which spawned hope for my future. That passion saved and changed me. I felt like a death row prisoner being released after a wrongful conviction. This freedom was sweeter than I could think or imagine!

The Struggle to Forgive

After entering this new relationship, I struggled to understand the kingdom principle of forgiveness. After receiving forgiveness from a merciful God, I faced a choice of obeying a simple request in the Lord's Prayer: "Forgive us our debts as we forgive our debtors."[4] How could I forgive those in authority over me who had not met my needs nor protected me? How could I forgive those who had purposely abused me and my loved ones? How could God expect me to forgive something that had caused so much pain? Did I have to forgive even though they weren't sorry?

The battle for who would maintain control over my life raged. Fellow believers who had more wisdom and experience in their relationship with the Lord than me explained the many benefits of forgiveness. As my vision cleared, I saw an exchange needed to take place. Initially, my heart screamed, "No!" but my mind was finally convinced I needed to fully forgive. My deep-seated resentment and desire for retaliation needed to be released through forgiveness. Freedom from my prison of pain came through giving up my right for revenge. I stopped drinking in the poison of bitterness while expecting it to hurt my abusers.

Forgiveness was the unexpected key that opened my prison.

Forgiveness was the surprising key that opened my prison cell. Granting an official pardon to those who had hurt me was the clear answer to my dilemma. I forgave my parents; I forgave my mother's second husband; I forgave everyone I held grudges against, even if they didn't ask for it. Going through this process was one of the hardest things I have ever done; but by placing the past behind me, freedom was birthed in my life. As I severed the ties of unforgiveness that were strangling me, I began to think more positively.

The secret power of God's forgiveness led me to repentance and into the hands of my Creator. Forgiving others gave me the power to live above the hurts of the past. I could breathe and not feel the overwhelming pressure of emotional hurts looming over me. The incredible freedom I enjoyed after forgiving was absolutely worth the effort.

The Act of Forgiving is . . .

Forgiving is like cutting the rope of a weight pulling us down.
Forgiving is the sword that slays the tyrant of hatred.
Forgiving protects against the plague of dysfunction.
Forgiveness is a shield against Satan's consuming, destructive darkness.

Forgiving is a weapon against the lies, wiles, and deceptions of the enemy of our soul.

Forgiving is a welcome relief after years of oppression and misery.

⸎

I found freedom by forgiving; you can too!

You might be asking, "How can I forgive the abuser of my children? How can I forgive those who betrayed me? How can I forgive the drunk driver who killed my wife?" The truth is forgiveness is ultimately your decision. Forgiveness can be granted as an act of your will; forgiveness is not a feeling. You can express forgiveness through silent prayer, saying it out loud to yourself, writing it out, or purposefully going to the person and forgiving them face-to-face. The important thing to remember is when you forgive, you free yourself.

The following true story is a powerful example of forgiveness. I met a woman at a training workshop and was struck by her wonderful smile and eyes beaming with joy and love. She told me the following account and gave me permission to share it with you. I have changed the names for privacy.

My husband, Jeffrey, left me after thirty-one years of marriage for another woman while on the island of Guam. He said, "I need a wife who's absolutely submissive to me."

I was angry when he filed for divorce and six months later married Sherry.

I went back to the mainland to live and be near our five grown children. God confirmed to me I needed to forgive him. So for six months, every morning, I said out loud, "Jeffrey, I forgive you and I love you. Sherry, I forgive you and I love you." I said it but didn't feel it.

Six months later, I said it and was surprised that for the first time, I felt it. I continued to say it out loud daily.

One year later, my daughter chose to be married on Guam; I was her matron of honor. During mass, the priest declared peace to the world and then asked us to move around the chapel declaring peace to each other.

Without hesitation, I went to Jeffrey and then to Sherry, saying to each, "Peace to you; I love you." They were surprised. I meant every word. I was freed through the power of forgiveness.

This story illustrates of the supernatural power of forgiveness to break chains and heal broken hearts. If we obey and forgive the person who hurt us, in spite of our natural inclination to do the opposite, we gain many benefits.

Forgiveness benefits the giver more than offender.[5] *Dann Stadler*

Forgiving can be one of the hardest decisions we will ever make. What do we do if we can't seem to make ourselves forgive? What do we do if unforgiveness keeps coming back even after we have prayed? How do we forgive if thoughts of revenge roll over and over inside of our head?

Prayer of Forgiveness

A prayer that frees us of the poison of unforgiveness might sound like this:

As an act of my will, I choose to forgive (name). I cleanse my heart and let go of all bitterness toward (name). I release a blessing on (name).

This pattern of forgiveness is all over the Bible. When old memories resurrect themselves, we choose to say it again. When we are tempted to take revenge, we decide to say it again. By holding to our resolve to forgive, let go, and bless, our hearts will change in time. Our emotions will eventually line up with our words.

Three important keys can be linked to the above prayer of forgiveness.

First Key

Forgiveness is an act of our will. To break free from the chains of unforgiveness, we decide to forgive as an act of our will even though we don't feel like it. Many of us do things we don't want to do every day. We pay our electric bill as an act of discipline even though our emotions might be drooling over a new phone. By making wise decisions, we can enjoy the benefits of a respectable credit rating instead of the hassle of a bill collector. The same is true in the spiritual realm. By making a wise decision to forgive in spite of how we feel, we can enjoy the benefits of being full of peace and joy instead of conflict and anger.

Choosing to forgive as an act of our will empowers us to be free instead of remaining slaves to our emotions. We become powerful by telling our negative emotions to be quiet. Even if we have not been taught how to forgive or not seen forgiveness modeled, Jesus commands us to forgive. If we don't know what words to say or how to walk through the process, we ask for the Holy Spirit to help us and do our best to obey. A friend or spiritual leader can be a huge blessing if they are willing to pray and assist us in this extremely freeing process.

Jesus encouraged his disciples, "When you are praying, forgive all those you hold anything against."[6] You have the freedom to forgive—choose forgiveness!

Second Key

We can choose to speak words of life over ourselves and others.[7] What we say trumps what we think inside our head. To see this principle in action, try this:

Think of something yellow. What are you imagining?

Now say, "The sky is blue."

What do you see now? Are you thinking of something yellow or blue? Most people will be thinking of a blue sky.

What we say becomes primary and overwrites what we were previously thinking. We can use the power of our words to set a new direction for our thoughts.

To eliminate a negative thought and replace it with a positive one, we use spoken words. Replace thoughts of unforgiveness with spoken words of forgiveness and blessing. Don't let thoughts make you a victim of hurtful memories. Speak your way to wholeness with words of forgiveness.

As we let go of our bitterness from the trauma caused by an unmet need, unhealed hurt or unsolved issue, we cut the past's power to emotionally hold us hostage. Unmet needs are those good things we feel should have happened to us in the normal course of life but didn't. Unhealed hurts are produced when something bad happens to us that, according to human logic, should not have happened. Negative situations we did not cause sometimes impact our lives. Unmet needs and unhealed hurts can result in unresolved issues when we are unable to process in healthy ways due to a lack of understanding. Forgiveness helps us to remove these hindrances so we can move forward.

How can you identify if you are struggling with unmet needs, unhealed hurts or unresolved issues? Ask yourself:

- Am I justifying being the way I am because of what has been done to me?
- Am I rationalizing, because of my past, I cannot be who God says I can be?
- Because of what I have done, am I denying I can do what God says I can do?

Unmet needs, unhealed hurts, and unresolved issues can seduce us into believing lies and developing unhealthy coping mechanisms. When we do not process traumatic experiences correctly, we might rationalize, justify, and accept wrong thinking and unhealthy behavior. Mired in our pain and fear, we can become paralyzed by those things we do not believe we can change, do not want to change or are afraid to change about ourselves. Our self-denial, self-reliance, self-protection, and self-defense prevent us from receiving God's truth. These create a wall between us and the voice of God.

If our response to trauma has created a barrier preventing us from seeing God as our protector and provider, we will not be receptive to God's Spirit, which brings our healing.[8] When we surrender control of our soul to God, we can receive revelation that exposes and removes all lies, wrong assumptions, and strongholds. When the Holy Spirit speaks truth directly to our spirit, it clears a path for us to receive our healing. When we move into a greater understanding and choose to forgive fully, freedom reigns in our lives.

If we refuse to accommodate our negative emotions and instead cooperate with the Holy Spirit to replace lies with the truth, we position ourselves for breakthrough and prepare ourselves for the third key.

Third Key

Blessing our enemy frees us permanently from trauma. We complete the forgiveness process by blessing the person who hurt us.

I have forgiven and blessed many people who have deeply wounded me. I have done this through gritted teeth, with tears streaming down my face and while my heart felt like shredded cheese. I forced myself to say the words out loud because I was not going to let someone else determine the course of my life. I was able to cut myself free from the weight of trauma sucking me under. As I heard myself speak the words, my mind was reprogrammed and past memories lost their power over me.

As we pray to bless someone who has hurt us, we elevate, spiritually and emotionally, above what has happened between us. No matter what someone did to disappoint or manipulate us, we determine the altitude of our path by controlling our thoughts and words. Forgiving, releasing, and blessing someone will bring us favorable rewards. Even if it is hard, we elevate through this cycle by dropping our backpack full of revenge rocks. The greater the offense, the greater our need to forgive.

Two books written on forgiveness have helped me renew my mind. Kris and Jason Vallottons' book *The Supernatural Power of Forgiveness*[9] is a moving book based on a heartbreaking real-life account. Jason shares details to bring the reader right into his painful struggle to forgive. His honesty and insights are touching. R.T. Kendall's book, *Total Forgiveness*[10] is a rich resource for those struggling with not being able to forgive their oppressor.

Choose to live life *bitter-free*! We can choose to be bitter or we can choose a better way. Bitterness makes for a pitiful life. We can choose to be pitiful or powerful but not both.

Freedom through Forgiveness

Over the past thirty years, the healing power of God's love and forgiveness has brought liberating release, true peace, and growing victory into my life. My liberation and restoration has taken time, effort, sacrifice, and determination. It has been worth it! For every investment I have made, I have been rewarded many times over. I now walk in a level of freedom I never thought possible. I believe in the supremacy of forgiveness in building relationships and resolving conflicts.

Walking in forgiveness, our second phase of transformation, gives us the power to neutralize every attack by our enemies. Our power to overcome pain and obstacles manifests when we choose to forgive in love. Forgiveness creates the emotional and spiritual atmosphere to remove the restraints that bind us. Forgiveness encourages the growth of healthy choices to love and be loved. Forgiveness is an investment in our journey toward wholeness. As we open our eyes to the beauty and power of forgiveness, we find freedom.

IRRESISTABLE INTIMACY

On my way to the secret place, coffee cup in hand, I know He is already waiting for me. The secret place is where I meet face-to-face with God. I crave our intimate time together when we join as one, and I hear His comforting voice and feel His touch.

I pull out yesterday's treasure, written on a scrap of paper stuffed in my Bible. I had clearly heard God's voice, full of compassion and tenderness, as a brother in Christ prayed these words over me,

> *The Lord wants to very slowly and gently hold you in His arms and rock you every day until you feel completely secure. He wants you to know He has all the time in the world for you. He will be quiet when you need quiet and sing to you when you need to feel and share joy together.*

It was as if God was speaking directly to the pain of my recent trauma.

Tears of healing leaked from my eyes and trickled down my cheeks as he continued,

There is nothing frantic, pressured or unpredictable here. He wants you to experience what it is like to live in a home where you can be embraced by His safe and nondemanding love.

My innermost hurts were soothed by what Father God, the Poet, whispered over me. This is what intimacy with Father God, my Best Friend, sounds like.

I spend time with Someone I can't see because Father God has proven Himself to me. I am never alone. Many times I recognize His voice as I read an inspiring book or write a well-crafted sentence. I hear Him in the robin's song and see Him in the rainbow. Every now and then I hear nothing but my own human thoughts, doubts, and fears, but I still know He is with me. My past experiences, born out of private time spent with God, have permanently transformed me into a person of faith.

After we accept His free gift and surrender our will to His lord-ship, we may enter into a passionate love affair with our Maker. By yielding our lives into the hands of an all-knowing, all-powerful, and all-loving God, we are refreshed. Instead of supposing God wants to manipulate mankind by dictatorial control, imagine He is intently waiting for us to speak His name. Our heavenly Father is jealous for each of us just as a groom is jealous over his bride. The Lover of our soul hungers to be in relationship with us.[11] We are always on His mind.

You are important to Him. You are always on His mind.

Let me tell you a secret about God many people never discover: God is seeking intimacy with every human being. Intimacy is the third phase of transformation. Every person is fashioned by our Creator to be in relationship with Him. He does not want a distant dictatorship where He makes all the rules and His children obey or else. He wants to know you *AND* He wants you to know Him. God wants to lovingly bond with you face-to-face. Your spiritual Father desires to talk with you spirit-to-spirit.

The third phase of transformation is about nurturing our relationship with God until we flow together. As we connect in a deeper way, our ears become tuned to hear and recognize His voice. This is one of the necessary and valuable benefits of intimacy.

We see many beautiful examples of vulnerability and intimacy all around us. When a mother kisses a baby's nose and snuggles her close, we witness the beauty of face-to-face intimacy. In the hospice ward, an elderly man holds his wife's hand and stares into her eyes communicating without words; this is a beautiful picture of spirit-to-spirit intimacy. With the honeymoon suite bathed in candlelight, they become one flesh as the bride bashfully offers her body to her soul mate; they experience a deeper level of physical intimacy.

All of these human models of intimacy are pictures of the spiritual intimacy God desires to have with you. You are the bride of Christ.[12]

Intimacy with God brings peace and contentment to your soul. Like the mother with her newborn, God wants to cuddle and snuggle with you. As a baby captures the heart of a mother long before birth, you were embedded in God's heart[13] before He knit you together in your mother's womb.[14] In much the same way as parents think of a baby's ten fingers and ten toes as miraculous, your Creator thinks you are astonishing and wonderful.[15] His Spirit wants to communicate with you through words, music, people, nature, and any means imaginable. He wants to love you in a very personal way, tailored uniquely so you can perceive His touch.

There is an important *why?* behind the secret of intimacy. Why do we need intimacy with God? Without it, we will be incomplete forever. Every person is created with a void, a God-shaped hole in their inner man only God's presence can fill. You will be amazed at how complete you feel through a permanent, authentic union with Him. In addition to making you whole, intimacy with God strengthens and enables you to overcome obstacles.[16]

You may need some time to wrap your head around this intimacy idea. It may help to remind yourself, *I am warmly welcomed into the loving presence of God.* Encourage yourself with, *God wants to spend time with me so we can get to know each other.* Jesus paid the ultimate price on Calvary, the place of His crucifixion, so you can experience the Father's presence freely. Give Him a chance to relate to you on a one-to-one basis and be prepared to experience the love He releases over you!

It doesn't matter what you have done in the past—God desires a relationship with you. Unlike the mistaken belief God is indifferent to your struggles and eager to punish you for every mistake, the opposite is true; God's love is reaching out to you. Your heavenly Father sacrificed His Son to pay the penalty for your sins instead of making you pay for them.[17]

Why would God make such a sacrifice?

God's love is bigger than a human mind can comprehend. His love *looks* like something. When He acts, His love is amazing. Love gives. Love sacrifices. Love covers. His love embraces you—the appealing parts, the ugly parts, and the parts you are desperately trying to hide. While human love may fail, God's powerful, infinite love never fails.[18]

The Limitless Resource

Instead of running from contact with God, we should be running to God, who is the source of everything we need. By coming into relationship with Him, we can walk away from the train wreck we have made and step into a new beginning. If we let Him, He literally takes us, remakes us, and gives us the freedom to live an abundant life.[19] Sometimes the pain of our past, demanding jobs, or dysfunctional family seem to suck the life right out of us. But when we run to Him, He revives us.

Intimacy empowers us to go through our personal struggles with the perfect Counselor. When He sees us struggle at the limits of our strength and willpower, God desires to partner with us in the fight and provide leadership and support. His principles are higher and His methods are more effective than ours and guide us toward success. Here's an example of one of God's higher principles in the food arena: Diets temporarily change the way we eat, what we eat or when we eat; fasting can permanently change the way we see food, our body, and our desires.

Intimacy transforms self-focus to Him-focus. Him-focus lets God impart how He sees us and how He wants to help us prosper and succeed.

What does Him-focus look like? Let's explore Him-focus by looking at food from another perspective. Wanting to come clean before Him, we might personally confess,

> *God, I need your help with this food thing. I keep failing over and over, gaining weight every time. I am fatter than all my friends and hate myself when I look in the mirror. As my life coach, what do you want me to do, Father God?*

God wants to lovingly sculpt how you see yourself to match how He sees you. He has your perfect shape and weight in mind. He might encourage you,

> *Give this battle to me. I am the one who made you. Not the mirror. Not Fashion Today. I will tell you what you should weigh. Stop measuring yourself against everyone else. No more depending on yourself. As you walk with me, I will complete this work in you. Everything that is important to you is important to me. Remember, I am Your Father and I delight in you.*

Can you hear His heart covering yours? He shoulders the load by lifting it off yours. Regardless of what happens, He is able to take good care of His children.

As we enter into a deeper, fuller relationship with God, spending time in His presence begins to transform us.[20] Dwelling with Him purifies out the junk and heals what is weak or diseased.[21]

As we praise and worship, read the Word, and practice the presence of God in our daily lives, we discover things we didn't know about our heavenly Father. What God loves and cares about becomes clear as we deepen our fellowship with Him. Just as we become more like the friends we spend time with, we become more like God when we spend time with Him.

Sometimes we think we know someone when in reality we don't. We have wrong assumptions about them that need to be corrected. As our intimacy builds through connecting with the real person, the truth replaces our wrong thinking. In the same way, time spent with God exposes the gap between who we think God is versus who He demonstrates He is. We find biases we thought were true because we heard them from well-meaning family or friends.

As a teenager, I repeatedly called out to God in my deepest times of need. Without seeing any evidence of His response, I allowed deep-seated anger against God to propagate in my heart. I assumed God was the source of the pain and abuse caused by other people, because I incorrectly thought He controlled everything everybody did. This gave me the impression God was undependable and unfair. Boy, was I wrong!

Distortions about God emerged as I blamed Him for the pain and suffering of growing up in an imperfect world where Julie was a victim of circumstance. Before I could comprehend God was the *only* source for my healing, my distortions had to go through an extraction process. Like decayed teeth with rotten roots, my false assumptions and accusations against my Heavenly Father needed to be identified, removed, and replaced with a correct image of God.

A friend and I thoroughly studied a thought-provoking book called *Please Let Me Know You, God.*[22] I uncovered distortions about God that were blocking the normal development of my relationship with Him. Here are a few indicators you may be dealing with a faulty image of God:

1. You feel separated from God and feel uncomfortable praying or reading the Bible.
2. You feel alone and angry at God for abandoning and neglecting you.
3. You don't go to church and don't trust Christians because they are hypocrites.
4. You think God expects you to be perfect and enjoys judging and punishing you.
5. You resent God for wanting your money.

As these distortions were replaced with the truth, I learned to trust God. I had to learn to line up my fickle feelings about God with my inner beliefs about God. Ignorance can prevent you from getting to know God and receiving His incredible love, mercy, and truth. Just as binoculars can sharpen our vision, encountering God's nurturing touch magnifies His true nature and brings His character into focus.[23]

Soon after I became a Christian, a good friend asked me, "Do you think God wants to give you good things?"

My automatic reply was, "No, I don't deserve them."

I was programmed to only expect rewards or words of affirmation as a result of hard work; I couldn't conceive why anyone would receive something they didn't deserve. As a nineteen-year-old, the concept of freely walking in abundance as a result of my heavenly Father's favor and blessing had never entered into my thoughts.

It took weeks for my friend to convince me it was in God's nature to give wonderful gifts to His children *and* God planned to give me delightful gifts solely because I was His beloved daughter. I eventually believed my heavenly Father wanted to give me good things. This was very different from my corrupted view of fatherhood.

We give Him what is broken and weak; He remakes us brand new. What a mind-blowing snapshot of how restorative His love is for us!

Don't let incorrect expectations formed during a hurtful period in your past determine your destiny. By dismantling the blockade of unmet expectations and needs, you can push forward in your amazing life makeover. Set your face like flint, stand firm in the face of expected adversity, and use the courage in your heart to blast that blockade open. Compelling truths and abundant resources are waiting for you.

Intimacy Requires Trust

Meaningful relationships are deepened when we choose to be vulnerable and entrust each other with our fears and failures, hopes and dreams. When a person trusts someone else with their tears or scars, the level of emotional intimacy is increased. This is a significant turning point in building relationship. In the movie *Scars That Heal*,[24] Dave Roever's wife lovingly kisses his scarred, misshapen face after it has been blown up in Vietnam. He weeps as his tormenting fear turns to joy when his wife assures him of her loyalty and affection. By this act of love, she affirms their relational intimacy despite the obvious challenges ahead.

Building intimacy with God requires vulnerability.[25] True intimacy with the Lover of our soul takes tremendous trust and commitment just like closeness does in our normal everyday human relationships. Vulnerability is an attitude which allows us to enter into relationships to be heard, seen, known, and loved without the need to hide our imperfections. Nothing on earth fills the void inside each human being like the intimacy with Father God. That's a promise!

This too shall pass.

Seasons of life come and go. During an extreme trial, a wise person once stated, "This too shall pass." We can act wisely even under distress by remembering this small but powerful phrase. As we partner with God and persevere, we are changed. As He plants His DNA in the soil of our weakness, His strength and character naturally spring forth within us. Difficulties develop patience, an expression of God's character, and draw out our best gifts. Using His dynamite strength, we rise to the occasion. When we stay connected through difficult times, the Lord teaches us how to access His strength and wisdom.

As He plants His DNA in the soil of our weakness,
His strength and character naturally spring forth within us.

Another benefit of trials is they expose our real level of intimacy with God. Our responses to stressful experiences reveal what we are thinking in our subconscious. Our need for God, His intervention, and His input becomes obvious as we cry out to Him in turbulent times. How many movies and books include a character muttering, "God, if you are real . . ." when faced with devastation?

During hardships and transitions, we discover the difference between having an intellectual knowledge of God and having encounters that expand our understanding of who He is. When we go through trials, peaks, and valleys with God as our ally, we can link our faith experiences together to form an accurate image of Him.

You may be asking, "How do I start being better friends with God?" The first steps may seem scary, but God is waiting for your *Yes*. Give your heart to the King of Kings, to the One who has loved you since He created you in the womb. Simply close your eyes and step into your first day as a new creation. If you are ready, join me in a simple prayer offering your heart to God:

Jesus, I need you. I have made lots of mistakes. I have not lived perfectly; I am a sinner. Would you please forgive me? Thank You for coming to die to pay the price for my sins. I am not whole without you. I need You to be Lord over my life. I accept you, Jesus, as my Savior. I surrender my heart and will over to You. I receive Your love and forgiveness. I am Yours and feel brand new. I am excited to see what happens now. In Jesus name, Amen.

If this is the first time you have accepted Jesus as your Savior, I rejoice with you in this life-changing decision. If you have prayed a similar prayer before, but don't know how to develop your relationship with God, I believe He has placed this book in your hands at the perfect time. It can be unnerving to interact with an invisible God, but He is waiting to show Himself to you.

Intimacy is About Relationship

The wisdom of the richest or most powerful men on earth is far below the wisdom of Almighty God. He is the Eternal Source of Truth. Everything we need is readily available if we will grab onto Him and depend on His input. The moment we cast fear aside and surrender to the Lord, we shift positions and enter into the family of God. When we join ourselves to the all-powerful, all-knowing Source, we have access to all of the wisdom and power of heaven.[26] The Holy Spirit is eager to be our tour guide as we traverse the maze of our life. He points us toward the right path every time.

When we seek out counsel from the Creator of the universe, He guides us concerning our finances, relationships, education, recreation, and our spiritual, mental, and physical health.

He is not looking for what is wrong with you, but wants to love you and give you good gifts. Many people are hesitant to let

God see their imperfections. Our flaws aren't a secret or a surprise; He knows already. Just like a house has many rooms, nooks, and closets, we have different compartments of our lives. God is a gentleman; God waits for us to invite Him into each room, nook, and closet when we are ready.

Trying to hide our problems, hurts, and fears from God doesn't make sense. Think about it. Why would you reject help or advice from the Creator of the universe? Why wouldn't you want His involvement in making improvements and decisions for your life?

After observing His loving nature and how brilliant He is, we willingly yield to His multidimensional work inside us. Our focus switches from outward religious expressions to producing internal transformative fruit. Instead of focusing on how we look externally, we focus on who we are in our inward parts. Instead of emphasizing outward traditions, we emphasize worshipping from the heart.

It's about a relationship, not religion.

Our relationship with God can't be based on feelings because feelings rise and fall like a roller coaster depending on our current predicament. When we are confronted by disappointments, He is the source of love, wisdom, and power we need to rise above our erupting emotional responses. If we trust Him, His peaceful presence naturally soothes every aspect of our chaos.

We are going to take a peek as a friend of mine shares about how she starts her day and receives from His source of love:

"Coffee time with Jesus" is what I call my early morning quiet time. It was easy to pour my morning cup of coffee, grab my basket filled with my Bible, prayer sheets, and miscellaneous books, and spend time with the Lord. Even though I was in the routine of praying and meditating on His Word, something was missing. Over time, I had lost sight of true intimacy, where my spirit connected to Jesus.

One day I sensed the Lord saying, How would you like it if you wrote an autobiography of your life and then your children read it over and over again, yet never really talked with you face-to-face? If they only read ABOUT you instead of choosing intimacy with you?

Ouch! I realized how easily I had fallen into just sleepily grabbing a devotional or my Bible and reading it without interacting with God. Sometimes I would pray convenient prayers, not really seeking the Lord on how to pray. I often prayed for people out of obligation so I could tell them later, "I prayed for you." That day, I heard God's heart; my eyes were opened. I changed my focus.

Coffee time is now "Connect to Jesus" time. Most days I roll out of bed on my knees and speak directly to the Lord. I like to praise and thank Him and then move out to the living room, with my basket and my coffee. I am still working on it. Every morning I look forward to shutting out the world and focusing on the Lord for our next intimate moment, just to bask in His love and His presence.

Victory Starts with Intimacy

Jesus, God's son, was very intimate with His Father and the Holy Spirit. Jesus spent time away from the crowds talking and listening to His Father on a regular basis. Jesus prayed at night, on mountains, and in gardens.[27] On purpose, Jesus refueled for full days of ministry being surrounded by the masses. By taking the time to soak in His Father's love, Jesus was prepared to meet the daily heavy demands of ministry life while being under constant scrutiny. He taught the principles of the Kingdom and demonstrated how to release the power of heaven on earth.

As disciples of Jesus, we saturate ourselves with God's presence to be ready for whatever comes our way.

Jesus was led into the Judaean wilderness for a time of testing.[28] He fasted for forty days before being enticed three times by Satan to sin. Jesus used His knowledge of the Word to reject the temptations

Satan presented.[29] As He quoted, "It is written . . ." to each appeal, He cast aside each seducing lie and defeated the enemy. When Jesus left the wilderness, He came out in victory.[30]

As we make over our lives, we need to be full of the Holy Spirit, internalize the truths in the Bible, and rely fully on God to come out of our trials and temptations victorious. Just as Jesus defeated direct temptations from Satan, we need to recognize we struggle against the same enemy. Our enemy, Satan, comes to steal, kill, and destroy us.[31] If we spend time talking and listening to God like Jesus did, we can come out in victory too!

When someone has a close and satisfying relationship with God, we recognize it in their conversations, prayers, and behavior. Intimacy shows up big time. Authentic relationship with God is easy to spot as it produces incredible fruit in a believer's life.

God is always with me, but how He makes His presence known is different every day. Sometimes my time in the secret place is over the top as we connect in worship and the Holy Spirit answers the cry of my heart for more. Some days His flawless truths jump off the pages of my Bible to prepare me in advance for what my day will hold. Occasionally my Conductor will sing a song that stirs the deep longings within my heart. There are also days when His peace and comfort descend as I quietly rest.

God is easy to find if we keep seeking. Discovering what works for us takes some exploration. Many people find music helps them to connect with God's Spirit. It might be slower worship music one day, silence the next day, and upbeat praise songs on another day. Varying the format, time or location can also help us hear God's voice. There are hundreds of topics in the Bible that address real human needs. Some days we might read one chapter or one verse; other days we might read out of an inspiring devotional or autobiography. Many ministries have resources for purchase on their websites or to watch for free on youtube.com.

We keep our time with Him fresh by mixing things up. Explore new opportunities to grow even if they are uncomfortable at first. Finding resources to use is not the problem; making time with God a daily priority is the challenge.

As a preview, I invite you to come to the secret place with me right now. We are going to ignore the world for a few minutes. As I go to my secret place in my home, find a place that feels right to you. Arrange a private getaway with God on your couch or a quilt-covered bed, outside by the trees, out in the garage, or in your man cave. By taking time to be alone with God, we can eliminate the distractions and hear His voice. Now I want you to slow down, close your eyes, breathe deeply in and out, and relax. Talk face-to-face with God by saying,

Father God, thank You for holding me in Your arms. I feel secure when You embrace me. Thank You, Father, I don't have to rush because You have all the time in the world for me. I never realized You like taking care of me. Thanks for being quiet when I need quiet and talking to me when I need advice. I am stressed out by dealing with things on my own. In You, Jesus, there is no need to feel frantic, pressured or unstable. Teach me, Lord, how to trust Your safe, nondemanding love. I receive all the good things You want to give me. Thank you, Jesus. Amen.

Welcome to intimacy, the third phase of transformation. Your answers are all hiding in the secret place with the Most High.[32]

A NEW, TRUE IDENTITY

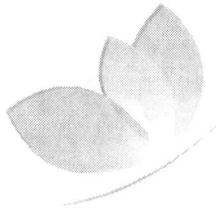

I strolled around the house, picking up toys my three young children had strewn about, muttering, "I'm invisible."

I didn't used to be. As a software analyst at Cray Research, helping build the fastest supercomputers in the world was exciting. I was appreciated by coworkers and complimented in yearly reviews. During a downsizing, I surrendered my grip on the career I loved to embrace being a stay-at-home mom.

Initially, I was thrilled to begin this new season. But the fantasy soon faded into a dull routine of never-ending tasks. Don't get me wrong, I loved being with my children. I really did.

It was hard being invisible after leaving a respected title and important projects. My three little ones demanded a lot, as all children do. My new title was unceremoniously "Mommy!" As I faced an endless parade of doing dishes, fighting mounds of laundry, and changing dirty diapers, I closed my eyes longing to find relief far away. My spouse's appreciative pat on the back was nice but didn't compare with the rave reviews I used to get at my 9-to-5 job.

Pushing over some clothes, still unfolded, and looking as neglected as I felt, I plopped onto the couch. "Who am I?" I asked myself.

A full-blown identity crisis had begun.

≋

The fourth phase of transformation is a process of allowing Christ and the Word of God to reform our identity. The identity of a person can be a fragile entity to manage. We can swing from one extreme to another, from fixating on our own importance to feeling devastated and insignificant. Whether it is from a positive change like having a baby or a negative change like losing a spouse, when we experience big shifts in our lives, it usually affects our identity. If our level of responsibility or status in life is altered, we may go through multiple life makeovers as we experience full or partial identity crises.

As you can probably tell from the scene above, my identity needed a facelift. As a home executive, I felt as if no one cared about what I went through. With the constant demands of caring for three children under five years old, I felt unappreciated. I also saw flaws in myself that had been covered over by the busy-ness of the working world and by a confidence based on good job reviews.

My prayer times were focused on dealing with the challenges of motherhood and asking God to change me from the inside out. I needed to get my value from the Lord and my dignity from how I served others, even when my sacrifices or struggles went unnoticed. To develop a servant-based nature, I needed internal transformation.

By experiencing an intimate relationship with God, we delicately but deliberately push our way out of our cocoon as a new butterfly. As a butterfly extracts himself from the cocoon, fluid is forced from his body and his wings gain the strength for flying. To lay aside our old self-image, we let our defenses down, allow hope to emerge, and cooperate as God creates a new identity within us. We transform from a fat fuzzy caterpillar who crawls into a beautiful mobile butterfly.

Our worth and value is securely grounded in the unconditional love and acceptance of the Lord.

The most important piece of spiritual clothing we can wear is God's love. Not human affection. Not physical, sexual passion. Not fond friendship. As we choose to put on the pure, selfless love flowing from the heart of our Maker, our Daddy, our King, this love becomes the source of our new identity. If His unconditional love seems to be a fantasy or a fairy tale, God wants to prove how real His love is. When we give God an opening, He assures us of His love through His gentle care and teaching.

God's type of love has the power to cover and wipe out the effects of multitudes of sins and abuses. His love is patient and kind; it is not touchy or rude.[33] Agape, the God kind of love, believes and hopes all things.[34] Agape love from the heart of Christ, our spiritual role model, is unconditional and eternal.[35] The Father's protective, graceful, embracing, empowering love woos us to Himself. His gentle touch entices us to let our guard down and open our heart to His pursuit.

A Miracle of Regeneration

After receiving Christ, my life became a miracle of regeneration. I received a new God-given identity on the inside of me. Boy, did my old one need replacing! As time passed by, I became convinced God could be counted on to supply a firm foundation to stand on. I learned to depend on His unwavering love in the midst of my mistakes and sometimes outright disobedience. The passionate love and uplifting voice of the Holy Spirit began to mold my identity and remake me into His image.

After I began to explore the concept that God's very essence IS love, I was able to make the next connection that as His daughter, His Spirit of love abides inside me. I finally accepted His love for me like a child. As His caring Spirit tenderly changed me, real and lasting transformation began to take place in my mind, will, and emotions. From the inside out, His affection helped me to accept myself.

Instead of automatically assuming lack in every area, I began to enjoy a wonderful prosperity of soul. I no longer operated from a poverty spirit but one of inner peace, joy, and deep happiness. My innermost man was nurtured by the empowering and affirming love of God. I saw potential in the opportunities around me. With hope, I worked to build a rewarding career. I connected to people. Love changed what I saw with my natural eyes and perceived with my spiritual eyes.

As Christians, our identity is based on how God sees us and how He describes us in the Word. Our identity is a combination of our personality, purpose, values, and character. We are created with a personality that uniquely expresses our individuality.

Our purpose, values, and character are molded under the guidance of the Holy Spirit. As disciples our purpose is defined by the great commission and the mandates of Jesus. Based on God's unchanging nature, our values are clarified and set into place as explained in God's Word. Our character is molded by applying the principles and promises in God's Word. In a lifelong process, our identity undergoes constant transformation through the ministry of His love. Neither the disappointments in this life nor the taunts spoken by other hurting people should be allowed to define who we are or who we will become.

Foundation Stones

Each question below highlights a key characteristic that is critical to forming a correct biblical view of ourselves. Each characteristic is a stone we use to build the foundation for our identity. We choose between two diametrically opposed ways of viewing ourselves. We choose between unhealthy foundation stones or healthy foundation stones. How we see ourselves and our sense of worth will directly affect our identity and future destiny.

Foundation Stones

- Are you messed up or a new creation?
- Are you driven to perform perfectly or free to live by grace through faith?
- Are you a condemned sinner or a much-loved saint?
- Are you a wounded victim or a victorious overcomer?

As we answer these questions, the challenge is to be brutally honest. Once we recognize we have an unhealthy foundation stone, we need to align our thoughts, words, choices, and behavior with God's vision of us. God sees us as new creations, saved by grace through faith, much loved-saints, and victorious overcomers. This can be quite a change from how we currently perceive ourselves.

We can all benefit from a reality check. This gives us the chance to reconcile the way God sees us versus the image we carry around inside our head or the identity we create with our words and actions. Through prayerful, honest evaluation of our daily responses, we can discover what we really believe about ourselves and then compare the results with how God sees us. God always has our highest and best in mind.

Let's say we have a friend going through a stressful time of adjusting to a job change, selling her house, aiding a friend going through cancer treatments, and trying to develop a new communication skill all at the same time. One day, while being overcome by the grief of her oldest child leaving home, she begins to sob uncontrollably. While trying to function under such pressure, this is quite a normal, human response. Because her mind reasons from the victim foundation stone, she condemns herself, "I am so weak. I can't help anyone else; no one can depend on me. Giving up is the only answer that makes sense." She criticizes herself even though she can quote the verse by heart, "I can do all things through Christ who strengthens me."[36] What has just happened?

Our friend has experienced a mini identity crisis by losing connection to her healthy foundation stone of being an overcomer who lives by grace. She can quickly recover once she recognizes her error, "Forgive me, Lord; I forgot who You created me to be. Thank You I am an overcomer in Christ and not a victim. Thank you for your grace when I am weak. Please help me with my grief and to stay healthy myself while I serve others around me."

As she processes her grief on the "hard days," she may need to take a short break to let God minister to her needs. On the "good days," the Overcomer in her will empower her to be Jesus to her ailing friend, deal with a difficult client at work, organize a messy closet or participate in team training. Christ, her cornerstone, will keep her identity in place while dealing with the highs and lows of daily living.

It may be enlightening to ask a spouse or close friend which answer best describes how we respond. They might be less biased in how they see us than we can be about ourselves. The most important thing to remember is if we are a Christian, God sees us as under grace, a saint, an exquisite new creation, and a definite overcomer through everything Jesus has provided.

Remember we are to love others as we love ourselves.[37] As we learn to love ourselves and give ourselves some breathing room to make mistakes, we will be able to pour out the same grace to others. It takes time to form a new godly identity. When we give ourselves time to grow and change, we will reach a beautiful, satisfying destination!

Are you messed up or a new creation? If we constantly view ourselves as messed up, we will focus on what we are doing wrong and not on what we are doing right. One of the fastest ways to kill the spirit of children is to focus on their mistakes and not encourage their gifts or dreams. Continually focusing on the negative will eventually produce damaging defensive thought patterns that prevent progress in our faith walk. The enemy and the world amplify every mistake we make, breeding condemnation into our spirit, to poison our self-image.

Focusing on the positive will position us to move forward. Inspiring teachers, for example, help paint a vision or define a goal for us to work toward. While we are in the process of learning, their encouragement enables us to press through the pain of not knowing what to do, where to go, how to act, who to trust or why something is malfunctioning.

I have a friend who used to teach violin to students in a wide age range. To draw out the best in her students, she would focus on something they were doing right. When she heard a wrong note or rhythm, she would address the mistake but only in a positive sense. "All the notes up to here were beautifully on pitch, but this one right here, try to make it sound like this (while she plays the right note) and the phrase will sound even better." She was able to plant the desired sound into each student's ears. By focusing on the positive, the student's understanding of the piece was developed while their self-image remained intact. As much as possible, emphasize the positive.

It is helpful to focus on cooperating with God and thanking Him for all we have been given as a new creation in Christ. The old life is gone; a new life has begun.[38] As a new creation, we receive energy from our Creator at the day's dawn. As crazy as it seems, there is new mercy for each day. God never runs out of kindness! We simply receive it and cooperate as God completes the new work He has begun in us.

God, our Creator, never tires of working through our messes with us and never runs out of patience. Freedom from condemnation is such a liberating concept. When we untangle ourselves from the stranglehold of self-condemnation, faith and hope propel us forward in our purpose. God wants us, as His special creation, to develop every skill and talent He has given us.

Are you driven to perform perfectly or free to live by grace through faith? It can be a challenge to transition from a performance-based mentality to a grace-based identity. If we continue operating according to the old incorrect thought patterns, we may feel the urge to perform, to try harder, or to be perfect to earn love. God wants to revamp our identity to be secure in our position as His son or daughter and confident His grace will empower us to grow and mature. Our Father encourages us to receive His mercy and accept His love, even though we are not perfect.

Perfectionism continued to drive and destroy me until
I realized I could NOT be perfect.

As a young believer, I almost killed myself trying to obey every commandment and striving to be the perfect Christian. The Holy Spirit gave me a new insight that I could not ever be perfect while living on Earth. Only God is perfect. God is perfect love. God does not expect us to live perfectly. We need to live in His grace, empowered by the Holy Spirit, and do our best each day. He is the author and the finisher of our faith;[30] we are not in this faith walk alone. We should delight in being His child, rest in His arms, and walk side by side with Him.

Trade sin-avoidance for love-consciousness.

We are human beings, not human doings. We need to move to a pattern of giving grace to ourselves and others when making mistakes. When shifting a grace-based mindset, we learn to accept we are not perfect, own up to our blunders, and avoid blaming others.

Many people judge other people by the results of their actions while judging themselves on their kind, good-natured intentions. What a double standard! It is immature to assess others by their voice tone and behavior while measuring ourselves by our well-intentioned motives and plans. We may tend to be a bit harsher with others than we are on ourselves because we naturally give ourselves the benefit of the doubt and the credit for trying.

If we monitor our thoughts and words, we can identify the motives we assign to others. Believing the best about others and giving them grace when they don't measure up will change how we see other people and improve how we relate to them in daily living.

Are you a condemned sinner or a much-loved saint? God wanted me to be comfortable with His gift of salvation that moved me back into a restored position as His daughter, a saint. A saint is not someone who is perfect; *a saint is someone who has moved into a royal status in the family of God.* The instant you accept Jesus as Lord of your life, you experience a change of position from a sinner to a saint, from being guilty to being declared innocent. Through salvation, we are born again, given right standing with God, and granted a new status of being His sons and daughters. Jesus' inheritance is in the saints; if you are a Christian, you are part of His family!

Our adoption as sons and daughters of the Most High is established when we become comfortable with who we are in Christ and accept our position as His beloved adopted children. As we begin to absorb this truth and begin adopting our new family title, how we view ourselves begins to mirror how God sees us. Saints are fashioned into the image of God as they are wrapped in the Father's love and adopt His nature.

Under stress, it can be difficult to maintain our identity as saints. A friend shared this example with me. The names have been changed for privacy.

Sitting in my car, I replayed a distressing conversation lodged in my thoughts. I replayed Stacy's allegations over and over.

"How dare you talk about my daughter behind her back? That is the sickest thing I have ever heard," accused Stacy.

"But I don't remember saying any of those things," I cried, trying to defend myself.

"Right now, I can't stand to even look at you."

"I'm sorry . . . I'll leave now," I uttered as I stepped out and left my best friend alone with her anger.

With my arms draped over the steering wheel, I faced multiple possibilities of how to respond. I initially entertained thoughts like, If I were a better friend this wouldn't happen. Why am I always the biggest screw up?

But then I remembered I am a much-loved saint. My response should be something like, "Jesus, thank you because you love me no matter what, and you will help me get through this and figure out how to respond in love."

As God's son or daughter, we learn to view ourselves through the eyes of the King, who also happens to be our Papa. Choosing to respond out of condemnation and guilt only leads to more problems. Maintaining our royal position as a saint gives us the ability to respond with mercy and confidence.

Are you a wounded victim or a victorious overcomer? Since gaining my freedom and victory, I am keenly aware of how many people live life with a victim mentality. They see their world, as I once saw mine, through the eyes of a defenseless target who is constantly under assault. Far too many people identify themselves as a wounded target and have no idea how to recover.

Many cloaked with a victim mentality cling to unhealthy protective mechanisms. In their delusion, they feel safe; while in fact, their self-protective mechanisms push them further away from the very people or experiences that could generate joy. Their concern over protecting themselves stifles their urge to reach out for the things that would bring them true healing or delight.

Stop waiting. Break out of this cycle at all costs. Dive in and start swimming.

If your ship doesn't come in, swim out to it!

We cannot always avoid being struck by some of the curveballs life throws at us. We can, however, choose our response.

Victims often sabotage even the beneficial things in their lives. Their negative words cancel out the blessings declared over their lives and prevent the provision God wants to give to them; but there are better options. We decide what to think, how we will identify ourselves, and how to proceed forward. A clear step-by-step description of how to shift from a victim mentality to an overcomer mentality is outlined in Phase 6: Power Struggles. By throwing off a victim mindset, we will be happier, healthier, and able to enjoy more positive relationships.

Negativity sucks the life out of every promising opportunity.

For those caught in an identity crisis, overhauling the way we see ourselves can be a long, arduous progression. Creating a masterpiece is never easy; but crafting a new sense of worth and value is a significant accomplishment. Keeping our focus on track during our transformation is important. We can't wait for others to do the work for us. Encouragement from others does help keep us moving, but ultimately our progress will be the result of the effort we put into it. With God's help, we will step beyond the victim mentality cage and onto the path to freedom and victory!

Overcomers focus on maintaining a good attitude and pursue relationship with others who are positive and encouraging. When added to our efforts, an atmosphere of positivity lifts us into a position of confidence and optimism. If we persist in filling our minds with the realm of what is possible through partnering with God, we will gain a strength of mind that is stunning.

Strong Convictions

Many people who have changed history had strong convictions and a strong identity. After years of facing vicious vocal opposition and cultural oppression, Martin Luther King Jr. was a history changer. Because he possessed a rock-solid identity and an unwavering set of values, Martin Luther King Jr. was able to lead a powerful civil rights movement resulting in permanent social change. He would not adapt his message even to those of his own race advocating violence. He did not waver in his message despite hardship and outright physical attacks.

A strong conviction combined with a secure identity keeps us moving forward, in spite of the pressure to stop our progress.

Winston Churchill was Great Britain's leader during World War II. His famous words, "Never, never, never give up!" have rung true for the generations following. His leadership was an expression of his identity and belief system that persevered in the midst of the purifying fires of nations warring for their survival. In the same way Winston Churchill was purified by wartime, we are purified, on a smaller scale, by our trials and tribulations.

Great men such as Martin Luther King Jr. and Winston Churchill stood strong during adversity. With a Christ-centered identity and Christ-based convictions, we can also stand strong during hard times and make a difference.

Our God-Given Identity

When teeing off, most golfers aim for the fairway and try to avoid obstacles like sand traps. As talented professional golfers like Tiger Woods demonstrate, success in the game of golf requires mental toughness. After landing in the rough, the golfer focuses on hitting the ball back onto the fairway and climbing back into the competition. The next spectacular shot is only a stroke away. Similarly, our identity takes a beating in the golf game of life, but like Tiger, we keep on swinging.

God's Word has thousands of positive statements to internalize to help form a new, stronger identity. Like using the correct pitching wedge, we can use the Word of God to take mental ownership of these truths and direct our path back on course. Feasting on the Bible-based declarations in Appendix A will enable us to correctly perceive and properly express ourselves.

God has so many wonderful things to say about you in the Bible! All of the keys you need are right at your fingertips if you are willing to start believing and speaking the right things. Believe how wonderful He thinks you are. Say this with confidence,

I am so glad, Father God, You think I am amazing and You are pleased with me as Your child. Thank You, Lord Jesus, I live under Your grace as a saint. Because You love and accept me just as I am, I love and accept myself. Thank You, Father God, I am a new creation and a victorious overcomer!

If you tell a five-year-old he or she can be a fireman or a pilot, he or she will believe you. As God's child, believe what He says about you, because our Papa God genuinely loves you just as you are. He enjoys being with you and encouraging you on the way to where you are going! Once you adopt the right foundation stones and step into your new identity, you will be well on your way to completing phase four of your makeover. Your launching pad toward your new identity in Christ is only a declaration away!

SUPERIOR MINDSETS

A monstrous twisted rope burns their hands as two teams scream and grunt, pulling it back and forth. Cheers roar from onlookers captivated by anticipation. One group sooner or later pulls the other group across the line into the mud; victory hugs and high fives abound. One group lives as victor for the day; the other waits for a rematch next year.

A similar tug-of-war takes place in our mind every day over who will control our thoughts. Will we entertain pessimistic attitudes that muddy our efforts to achieve our goals or will we dwell on the constructive ideas that build us up and empower us to step forward?

The fifth phase of transformation is implementing a new and improved mindset shaped by the Holy Spirit. Our thoughts are powerful because they determine our ability to bear fruit. We are encouraged in the Bible to think about what is excellent, worthy of praise, true, honorable, right, pure, beautiful, and respected.[40] Filling our minds with these things will keep us in line with the mind of Christ. What we focus on we give power to.

Do you want negative fruit or positive fruit in your life?

Negative thoughts become negative words →

Negative words become negative actions →

Negative actions become negative habits →

Negative habits bring negative fruit into your life.

Positive thoughts become positive words →

Positive words become positive actions →

Positive actions become positive habits →

Positive habits bring positive fruit into your life.

Opposing thoughts *"Yes, I can and No, I can't"* sometimes war against each other in our mind and become a tug-of-war in our psyche. Ideas that are allowed to take root will influence our words and behavior and will determine whether we regard ourselves positively or negatively.

❈

"Trust me! My friend's practically a snowboarding expert; we should be able to catch some air. The powder is gonna be sweet on the black diamond runs!" Jim exclaimed.

Mentally rewinding the movie of the last twenty years, Jim's mom couldn't recall one memory of Jim ever strapping on a snowboard. Having witnessed his fear of heights in the past, she protested hotly, "What? You've never snowboarded before. Black diamonds are steep and dangerous. You never know what could happen if you have an accident. Do you have a death wish? If you decide to do this anyway, would you please text me after your first lesson to let me know you're still alive?"

If you were Jim, would you listen to the voice coming from your inner passion or the fearful voice coming from outside? Would you listen to the *I can* voice or the *be afraid* voice?

We face the same dilemma during an incredible life makeover. Pushing past the fear begins the moment we determine nothing is going to stop us; we rent the equipment and schedule a lesson with our friend. If we are willing to endure the wipeouts and lessons, we will soon be snowboarding down the black diamonds, pumped full of adrenaline, risking life and limb. Imagine our heart's cry as all of our courage, hard work, bruises, and determination pay off as our makeover goes airborne and we feel fully alive.

Securing Our Thought Life

Have you ever watched planes coming and going at a busy international airport and wondered how they keep them all straight?"

Airports and Runways

Our thought life is like an international airport with pictures, sounds, perceptions, and sensations traveling through established runways. Airports have three levels of security concerns: the airspace above, the aircraft arriving and leaving, and the runways themselves. To keep our thought life secure, we set boundaries and control our responses to multiple environments, relationships, and input and output streams.

Our existing thought patterns are like the runways of an airport. Like asphalt runways, good thought patterns need to be repaired and maintained. Some of them are old and need to be replaced. All of the illegal airstrips should be purposely, permanently demolished. New runways are built to receive truth. Our mind, our airport, is designed to operate according to God's ways and purposes.

When we realize we are entertaining a thought that is not helpful, we resist that thought. Planes carrying destructive thoughts are diverted and denied the right to touch down on the landing strips going into our mind. After banned runways are out of service, we build new runways by carefully selecting what principle to concentrate on and declare. The goal is to only allow planes carrying uplifting, truthful cargo near our landing field.

Identifying the wrong runways and building new ones can be challenging but very rewarding. During high school, I spent many nights with my aunt and uncle. They were convinced I was prepared for college, even though neither of them had gone. My old thought recordings of, *I'm stupid; I am so stupid. I'm not good enough; I will never be good enough. I'll never amount to anything* . . . needed to be demolished. After my aunt and uncle helped me to identify which runways ought to be destroyed, I was able to reject such lies. I did attend a four-year liberal arts college and loved every minute on my way to a computer science degree!

To keep us from looking to God as our answer, the enemy tries to fill our minds with negative thoughts and lies; he attempts to overload our emotions with condemnation, unforgiveness, and rage. Satan wants to destroy our identity and keep us enslaved with his depressing voice. His whispers of ridicule breed discouragement and instill a live-for-the-fun-of-today mentality with nothing to anticipate. He uses deception to destroy our motivation to start over or make an effort. As God's children we learn to recognize this ugly voice and aggressively resist it.

What kind of illegal runways are operating in your mind? Do you have runways built for replaying the traumatic memories of the past? Is the enemy constantly tormenting you with thoughts of rejection and failure that come gliding in on old taunting pathways? Do you hear constant condemnation, criticism, and life-destroying curses landing day after day? For a successful makeover, follow the leading of the Holy Spirit, destroy unwanted, out-of-date runways, and only allow legal productive traffic to descend.

Removing Illegal Runways

An illegal runway is when we allow a long-held pattern of thought to continue because we don't recognize it as faulty. Through conversational prayer, we gain God's perspective of what is true. He loves to have conversations with us; we ask Him questions and take note of His revelatory answers; we praise Him for the good things in our lives and listen for His response.

We need to know how to recognize God's voice. God's voice will never violate His Word. Once we hear His voice, we should feel the peace of Christ in our heart. Sometimes we may hear a confirming word through the counsel of a friend or a prophetic word. The Holy Spirit leads us into truth through many avenues, which may include divine connections or timing. As the Father's children, we learn to hear His voice as we go to Him in prayer and focus on listening.

Let's look at an irrational fear of confronting others about difficult situations as an example of an illegal runway. We can ask God three questions to help us overcome the fear of confronting. These questions can be adapted to any illegal or negative pattern of thought you want to replace.

First Question

First we ask, "*Father God, why am I allowing fear to control this situation?*" We may hear answers that sound like excuses: Fear is shielding me from the anguish I would go through if I had met with them. Fear is keeping me from saying the wrong thing and making the situation worse. Fear protects me from bad things. All of these are based on imagined negative outcomes in the future.

Recognizing when we are being hampered by fear, what we are afraid of, and what we think fear is protecting us from is the first step to breaking free.

Second Question

Next we ask, *"Father God, what am I allowing this fear of confronting to steal from me in this situation?"* The answers to this question may be harder to hear. If we don't hear anything, we can ask a different question, *"What blessings are being delayed because of my fear-based paralysis?"* or *"What is my indecision preventing me from seeing or doing?"* When we delay taking action because we are afraid, we need to see things from a fresh perspective.

As we read our Bible, pray, and listen for His voice over the next few hours or days, we may hear, sense or feel God speaking to us. The answer may sound like any one of these: *Fear is interfering in your family relationships and preventing peace. Fear is keeping you from seeing what is possible if you act in faith. Fear is hindering you from coming into My Presence. Fear is tormenting you and stealing your identity and destiny.* When we notice our quality of life is being disturbed by torment, we can push anxiety aside and run into the peace, presence, and freedom of God.

Third Question

Lastly and most importantly, ask God, *"Father God, what do I need to do to break out of the control of fear?"* It is imperative we do not partner with fear nor entertain, confess or agree with it. We can always ask the Holy Spirit to increase our faith so we can operate from the right mindset. As we step out in faith, He guides our steps and speaks into our spirit.

What comes into our mental airport is what will leave our airport. Thoughts that are allowed into the airfield of our mind will one day produce words departing out of our mouth that will frame our future. It is worth our time to take an inventory of what we are allowing to enter on our landing strip. By putting some healthy boundaries in place, we prevent terrorists from taking over our airspace! Similar to the lights of a runway approach system, our mental runways are kept secure by the Word of God and illuminated by the Holy Spirit.

Our thoughts produce words and actions that lead us toward blessing and prosperity or toward cursing and poverty. We decide what we will think about. Many people allow others to program what they should think about and how they should live. For some people, this pattern of living is the road of least resistance; however, they also reap the results of someone else's programming. To avoid the world's programming, which results in depression, sickness, and broken relationships, we bring our thoughts into alignment with Christ and under obedience to the Word of God.[41]

Handcuffing Toxic Thoughts

In the beginning of my makeover, I realized I was being ruled by my old thought patterns and negative emotions. I needed to bring them under my control, not suppress them or indulge them. There was a direct connection between my deceptive, old mindset and my emotional ups and downs. When I slipped back into my old thought patterns, I would lapse into a depression and imagine abandonment all around. My thoughts spiraled down, out of control, overwhelming me. But then totally out of the blue, something positive would happen, and I would rebound and get back on track.

I continued to grow by reading and hearing the Word of God. Its truth began to set me free as I learned to evaluate my thoughts through my new lens. Where my thoughts were opposite of the Word of God, my human reasoning began to slowly bend toward the truth. This bending grew to be so prevalent a friend and I chuckled as we exclaimed in unison, "If it feels weird, it must be normal; therefore do it!"

Hurting people hurt other people.

One of the hardest times for me to handcuff my toxic thoughts was when someone hurt me on purpose. When I faced such painful situations, I tried to remember hurting people hurt other people. This little phrase came in handy while I learned how to handle unfair consequences and rude, demanding people. Its wisdom motivated me to peer inside the mixed-up minds and misguided emotions of people who hadn't treated me properly. I probed for details concerning the person behind the act. What was their life like? What was their inner motivation? What wounds did they carry on the inside? Were they one of the *hurting people*?

Once I glimpsed their pain, I could see how their pain transferred into my life. It was similar to how the baggage and destructive lifestyles of alcoholism and physical abuse pass on from one generation to the next. Suddenly, forgiving those who had hurt me became doable. Rejecting my toxic thoughts was not simple by any means, but it was easier when I envisioned the offenders as humans with deep-seated hurts and needs. Acknowledging the humanity and pain of others in this way moved the act of forgiving from the impossible realm to the difficult but possible realm. I learned how to exchange revenge for forgiveness, which allowed a greater level of freedom to manifest in my relationships and surroundings.

How do we reject a toxic thought? When we hear the words *I'm stupid* repeating in our head, it is time to take this falsehood captive and challenge it. Take control by saying,

"I reject that thought. I am smart; I study and am able to learn many things quickly."

It will probably take several cycles of rejecting the negative thought and replacing it with a positive idea, but over time the new confession will reprogram our old response.

For more information on removing toxic thoughts and replacing them with positive ones, Dr. Caroline Leaf gives many examples in her books, *Who Switched Off My Brain: Controlling Toxic Thoughts and Emotions*[42] and *Switch On Your Brain: The Key to Peak Happiness, Thinking and Health.*[43]

Making Good Decisions

When we practice disciplined, positive biblical meditation, we set the groundwork to make powerful declarations. These affect everything in our sphere of influence. When the time comes for us to act on our vision, the foundation our dreams are built on will be tested. If our foundation is built on the rock of Jesus, it will endure during the storms of transition and opposition. If our foundation is built on the sands of public opinion or self-interest, it may easily buckle under the pressure. By meditating on eternal truth, we set a secure foundation to build our dreams on.

How do we permanently change our thought life? One word: *meditation*. Meditation is a powerful biblical concept. Meditation is the practice of turning a thought over and over until it becomes part of our very being. There is power in the habit of focusing our attention on a new idea or principle. Throughout the day, week, and month, we meditate to renew our mind with the Word of God. If we meditate on the negative that could happen, we descend into worry. Unfortunately, negative thoughts can become the ruling party in our lives just as easily as positive thoughts can.

To meditate means to ponder, mutter, speak or study. Committing ourselves to the practice of biblical meditation will bring about the desired result every time. Deliberating on the Word of God always leads to wise dealings and good success.[44] On the other hand, meditating on worldly ways leads to foolishness and failure. In order to change our thought life, we take a concept out of the Word of God and think about it and talk about it, think about it and talk about it. Repetition is needed until the truth finally takes over and ultimately brings forth the corresponding actions that express the truth.

Meditation is part of the prescription for receiving God's blessings and His works. Meditating on the positive reminds us of who God is. We should emphasize the miraculous things He has done in the past and He is ready to do now. Focusing on past disappointments, complaining about how hard things are, and entertaining unbelief will hinder God's blessing and favor. With positive thoughts and words, we can choose life and claim our rightful inheritance. In our inner self, we are what we think with our minds and say with our lips. We all live by the fruit of our thoughts and words.

The real battlefield is in the mind.

Developing Decision Muscles

As we go through the makeover process, I propose developing what I call *decision muscles*. Developing our decision muscles will fortify our mind and willpower so we do not give way to negative outside pressure. If we increase our awareness of what is in our airspace, it is easier to keep track of negative mental traffic and limit its influence. Once we learn to stay focused in our thought life, our words begin to agree with our meditations. This strength of mind restrains us from taking undesirable actions and supports follow-through for beneficial actions.

Our lives can change for the better by keeping our thoughts, words, and actions set on the Word of God. Through the power of meditation, one thought can become a faith-filled profession that can result in powerful decisions. These decisions can spark actions that determine our destiny and impact the lives of those around us. Our transformation can spark hope in others that their physical health, relationships, mental health, education, job or future can be improved.

A ship can be turned by the helmsman with a very small, strong rudder. Our thoughts are like the helm of a ship. Our words and actions perform the rudder action. Our thoughts, like an officer of the watch, determine the direction we will sail while our words and actions essentially turn our lives in the desired direction. The pressure of the water pressing, pressing, pressing against the rudder will decisively turn an enormous battleship. Submitting to the laws of physics, the ship will rotate. As we submit our thoughts to the process of meditation, our battleship will swing in a newly determined direction.

There is more power in our thoughts than most people realize. The battle for every makeover begins in the mind. The fifth phase of transformation is critical because the right thought life is the key to right living. Once we have established intimacy with God and learned to extend forgiveness under duress, we have prepared to wage many tug-of-war sessions in the battlefield of our minds.

As we handcuff toxic thoughts and purposely set the foundation for kingdom thoughts to take over, the soil of our mind and heart becomes rich with potential. A clean heart and a surrendered will are the perfect environment for the Holy Spirit to nurture a higher vision for our lives. I can see the wildflowers of your makeover growing already!

POWER STRUGGLES

A rambunctious two year old arches his back and throws his body on the grocery store floor. With arms and feet flailing, his screams pierce the atmosphere, "I want some caaannndy! Give me some caaannndy!"

Wearing an embarrassed, exhausted expression on her face and using her most convincing *now-listen-up* tone, his mother coaxes, "Stop screaming right now. Do you want a time out? If you don't stop . . ."

Looking away we think, "I know just how she feels. I remember when . . ."

As reluctant observers of this nerve-racking clash for domination, we have witnessed one of mankind's oldest struggles for control. From the day we are born, we want to be in control. But in control over what?

It is helpful to have the understanding God creates each person as a three-part being. We live in a body; we have a soul; we are a spirit. Once we comprehend how the three separate parts interact, the intricate system which guides our thoughts, decisions, and even inner conflicts begins to make sense.

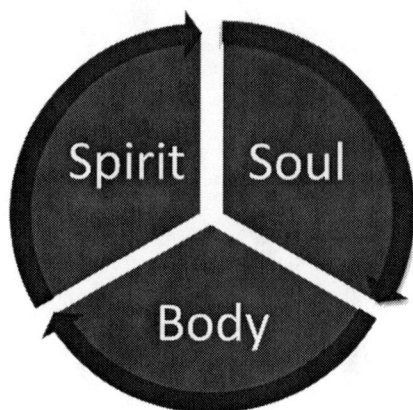

When we accept Jesus as our Savior and become a new creation in Christ, a new, perfect spirit is planted on the inside of us. This spirit is full of the Holy Spirit and in complete agreement with God. While this is an exciting, life-altering change, our soul man needs to listen and align with a new spiritual headship. The power struggle arises as we discipline our thoughts, words, and actions. As we watch and pray, our spirit will be strengthened; we will be less likely to give in to temptation. Over time, our spirit is able to exert more and more influence over the soul realm.

Ultimately, the objective is to have our spirit man be the main influence over what we think, feel, and decide.

Learning to follow the leading of the Holy Spirit and control our soul is the goal of the sixth phase of transformation. As Christians, we are meant to be in charge of our responses; we are not meant to be the slave of our responses. Sometimes our body hungers for something that does not agree with what our spirit wants—a physical addiction, for example. Sometimes our emotions in our soul want to be in charge over our spirit—depression, for example. As we gain mastery over our body and soul, our behavior and character come into closer alignment with our new spirit. Freedom from addictions and freedom from depression are two powerful examples of winning the power struggle.

After we get saved, this power struggle between the three parts of our soul competing with the new dictates of our spirit can breed anxiety and confusion. The concept of taking control of the spiritual content of what we think, say, feel or do is foreign to many people. In general, most of society looks to the media or their friends to tell them what to think and feel. As Christians, we are responsible for the difficult task of taking simultaneous charge of our body, soul, and spirit.

To fully take charge of our soul realm, it is helpful to recognize the three parts of the soul. Our soul realm consists of our mind (thoughts and imaginations), emotions, and will (final decisions).

Our soul train consists of our mind, will, and emotions.

Think of the three parts of the soul like a train. Our wills and thoughts are the train engines and cars that determine where we will go and how fast we will arrive there. With smart decisions, based on positive, powerful thoughts, we make progress toward our goals and dreams. Since our emotions can be fickle, they should be kept in the train's caboose.

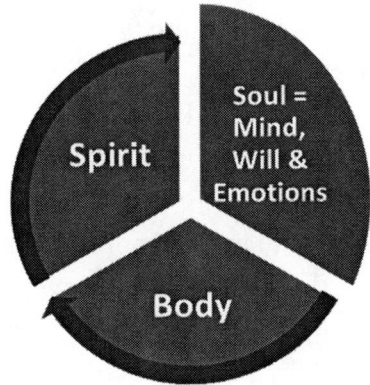

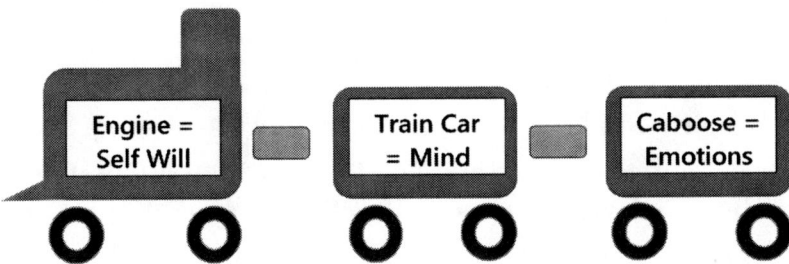

Sometimes the mind, will, and emotions disagree with each other, which causes confusion or uncertainty. After we become a Christian, we begin to notice some of our old thought patterns make us uncomfortable. Our new spirit on the inside sends us signals when our thoughts do not align with our new kingdom paradigm. Instead of conforming to the thought patterns of this world, our minds are transformed and renewed by reading the Word of God. Before Christ, our emotions ruled the day; after Christ, we learn to discipline our emotions to stay in the caboose.

When chaos erupts in our soul, we can stay in command of our faculties regardless of the circumstances. How do we control such chaos? By asking God about it, finding out what the Bible says about it, and seeking out godly counsel, we can identify which parts of the soul need to be realigned so we can be at peace within ourselves. By cooperating with God to align our thoughts, words, and actions to His will, we develop our spiritual muscles to properly exert our spiritual authority. In the end, we make better decisions according to the kingdom of heaven. Obedience to God's instructions will bring His provision, protection, and blessing.

Aligning Our Will

Making up our mind is a valuable and necessary part of the human experience. While we are fashioned with the priceless gift of a free will, it comes with the price tag of responsibility.

To grow into healthy and whole individuals, our free will needs to be disciplined and protected. God's way of doing things is perfect. To gain the benefit of His wisdom, we align our will with the Holy Spirit and keep it set. It doesn't help us if we bend the rules to suit our weaknesses. We go through an important process to learn how to govern our *will* with self-discipline. Without self-control, our decisions can get us into a terrible cycle of gluttonous self-indulgence and destructive addiction.

Unfortunately, we may also get into situations that require us to defend against manipulation, intimidation, and even domination by other people. An assertive show of willpower prevents dysfunctional people from exerting harsh control over us. We protect our interests by strongly taking action as guided by the fruit of the Spirit.

Our mind, will, and emotions will fight against God's Spirit inside of us until our soul becomes renewed by the Word and learns to submit to Christ. To do this, we take every thought captive by comparing it to what the Bible says so we will not be manipulated by immature thoughts rising within our *mind*. We limit the effects of any negative feelings and refuse to let our *emotions* rule us.

Taking Thoughts Captive

Makeovers require taking every thought captive. Just like a knight develops his skill with a blade for battle, we train ourselves to wield self-control in the battle of discerning life's competing voices. How do we take every thought captive? There are three basic steps.

Identify the Voice

The first step is to *identify* the source of the voice. Whose voice is it: God's, Satan's, or ours? We make fewer mistakes if we don't act right away on thoughts we have, but ask, "Where did this thought come from? What does this thought line up with?" While we don't make decisions by our

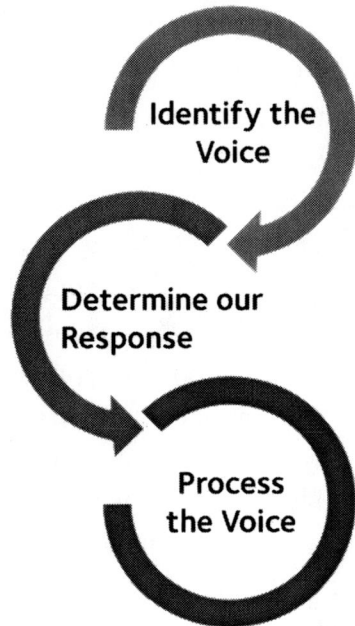

Identify the
Voice

Determine our
Response

Process
the Voice

feelings, it is helpful to be aware of how this thought makes us feel. Our conscience or our internal "knower" can give us important clues.

Identifying the voice gets easier the more we do it. The closer we get to God, the easier it is to tell His voice. God's voice is loving and affirming. Our adversary slyly plants accusations and guilt to make us cringe and shrink away from God. Voices of self-criticism, doubt, and fear can also come from our old, unrenewed patterns of thinking. It is always wise to ask the Holy Spirit to help us pinpoint the source and see if it agrees or disagrees with what the Word says. Sometimes it helps to get a godly friend's advice on whose voice it is.

When we are in the middle of our makeover and trying to change our behavior and way of thinking, we will make mistakes. When we mess up, tension can rise within us. Our conscience is pricked. In this state of unrest, it is important to know the difference between the conviction of the Holy Spirit and condemnation from the devil, ourselves, or others.

Just as earthly parents correct their children out of love and concern, God corrects things that are wrong in our lives because we are His beloved children. If we respond from a position of healthy relationship, His correction of sin brings conviction. We experience relief when we admit what we have done and invite the Father to help us take responsibility for any wrong actions.

On the other hand, if we feel condemned when we blunder, we should reject any exaggerated judgments coming from the kingdom of darkness that try to magnify what we did wrong. If a "voice" makes us feel so condemned we want to shrink back from God, it isn't from God. There is no condemnation for those who are in Christ Jesus.[45] God's correction is always accompanied by a loving voice drawing us back to Him.

If a thought makes us so ashamed we want to hide our face, we know it isn't from God because God does not use shame to correct His children.[46] We may be embarrassed because we have made a mistake, but our heavenly Father is ready to forgive, correct us in love, and protect us from further exposure if possible.

If a thought provokes fear, we need to carefully analyze where the fear came from. Fear isn't from God; God urges great men and women in the Bible, "Do not fear."[47] Satan uses lies to breed fear in us after we make a mistake. Sometimes an instruction from God can challenge us and provoke an unhealthy fearful response. This is when we need to wait and use discernment. The only healthy fear is the fear of the Lord. God is wanting us to trust Him and act in faith when challenged or disciplined.

Feelings of condemnation, shame or fear do not come from God. We might bring them on ourselves or allow the world's system to put them on us; they are not from God. When we make a mistake and feel separation from Father God, He is always looking to bring us back to Himself, hear our confession, restore right relationship with Him, and help us reconcile with others.

Early in our faith walk, conviction may seem like condemnation if we are receiving it through an old lens or filter; but conviction will always lead us toward the Source of Truth. Condemnation leads us toward captivity and away from God. With time, we learn to tell the difference between the two.

Determine Our Response

Once we have determined the source of the voice, the second step in taking our thoughts captive is to *determine* our response whether to accept or reject it. If the thought is from God, we embrace it, even if we don't understand it at the time. If the thought is from Satan, we resist and reject it. If the thought is from inside ourselves, we determine:

1. Is it a godly, positive or neutral thought that can be accepted?

or

2. Is it an ungodly or negative thought that needs to be expelled?

If we are having trouble distinguishing between the two, it helps to talk with God about our thoughts. Sometimes when we share our thoughts aloud and hear them with our ears, we are able to recognize lies that seemed reasonable when they were rolling around in our head. Listen to God's Spirit; His answer is inside us.

By thorough, purposeful evaluation, our goal is to prevent any speech or actions yielding negative fruit. We want to speak and behave in a manner that cultivates mouthwatering fruit, not rotten fruit.

Process the Voice

The final step of taking a thought captive is to *process* the voice: accept and repeat it OR reject and replace it. If we are going to accept our thoughts, we can consciously repeat and meditate on them to make them permanent. If we discover our thoughts are not in line with God's Word, we counterattack; we reject and replace them.

What does a counterattack sound like? If the voice came from an old, unhealthy thought pattern, I reject it by saying, "I will not think that thought." All thoughts not in alignment with the Word of God should be rejected. *I will not think that thought* is the most powerful phrase I have used in making over my thought life. It might sound like this:

I will not think that thought.
I reject the lie my parents did not love me.
I will not cooperate with the spirit of rejection.

Once I stop agreeing with the thought and reject it, I replace it with thoughts that align with God's way of thinking. Here is an example of a more positive response:

Thank you, Lord, for loving me and having a great plan for my life.
Thank you, Lord, my parents did love me to the best of their ability.
Meet their needs, Lord, and bless them.

This prayer shifts the control in my mind from the lie I was believing to the truth God loves me and so do my parents. By my counterattack, I construct a firm platform on which to build a better relationship with God and my parents.

Many times Satan's voice transmits lies, prompted by the spirit of fear, into our minds. Some people perpetuate the fear of the unknown by saying things like, "Oh, you had better not risk starting your business; the stock market could crash anytime." The fear of a negative response may keep us from saying hello to our coworkers or neighbors. If we yield to Satan's voice, fear can bring panic, paralysis, and passivity. From Genesis to Revelation, God encourages men and women of faith with the words, "Do not be afraid."

The spirit of fear introduces a mixture of lies to distort your identity and divert your attention from accomplishing your purpose. Maybe you think you are not smart enough to go back to school. That self-defeating lie probably came from something someone said to you years ago. Can you see the fear and fabrication behind the lie? These falsehoods keep you in a repressed job or in dysfunctional relationships because you believe you lack the capacity to go after your dreams or save yourself for a healthy and satisfying relationship. This lie promotes a feeling of worthlessness and stifles creativity and movement.

Lies based in fear can keep you from taking
steps toward your makeover.

God is our source of strength and dynamic working power for this battle. If we are buried under deception, He will help us dig our way out. When fear causes paralysis, we can move again as He energizes us. If we have to, we will claw and scratch our way out. With Him by our side and speaking constant encouragement, we fight our way to glorious freedom and break the enslavement caused by lies implanted in the past.

As we submit ourselves to God and resist the devil's way of thinking and doing things, the devil will flee.[48] When we actively fight against the enemy, we win in the long run. Satan and his demon hordes will slink off until another opportune time. There are times in our lives when if we do not fight back, Satan will not vacate the premises and our lives remain under his negative influence.

Every voice powered by the kingdom of darkness tries to lure us in, pull us down, and place us underneath their jurisdiction. Under a spirit of deception, we mistakenly think we are doing what we want, but we are falsely coming underneath Satan's control and being manipulated. It can be hard not to play his game of buying stuff and mindlessly watching TV or movies to fill our void and avoid our nagging problems. The only way to break free is to align our lives with truth and light. Freedom comes by learning to see and think for ourselves.

Believing lies about yourself destroys self-esteem and self-confidence.

If we listen to lies about our identity, abilities, or future, we live with low self-esteem and a lack of self-confidence. Our adversary uses seductive lies and sly deceptions to keep us powerless, silent, and trapped. Lies are powerful and cause destruction everywhere they are allowed to multiply. Every smart game plan works to identify and reject the enemy's deceptions as soon as possible. Once they are exposed, we counterattack with words of truth. Praying verses out of the Bible over yourself is effective because declaring the truth out loud gives us power to bring forth results.[49] The longer we allow deception to spread, the larger the mess to clean up and the less time and energy we have left to work on our incredible life makeovers.

It is easy to believe the lie people don't like us. This stems from another lie we aren't lovable. As God's love reveals to our spirit how wonderful He thinks we are, our inner worth increases. We start to like ourselves. God's approval gives us the security and stability we need in order to receive the love people want to give us—they aren't just faking it.

Replacing lies with the truth is vital to a successful makeover.

Removing lies is a powerful part of your makeover preparation and empowerment. Take a few minutes to sit in a quiet place with a pencil in hand. Simply ask God, "What lies am I believing about myself?" Do any of these resonate for you?

No one cares.
I don't belong here.
I am afraid of the future.
I am stupid to think I can change.
I can protect myself better than God can.
It's too hard or too late to change because I'm too tired.
I should ignore Satan because he might notice me and attack.
I will get farther by myself than by giving my life over to God.

If you are able to identify a lie you are believing about yourself, that is great news. This means you are halfway there. It is time to remove every toxic thought. As an example, let's say you are believing a lie you are stupid. Take charge and say,

Father God, thank you for revealing I am believing a lie about myself. I reject the lie I am stupid. I will not believe I am stupid any longer. I will not base any decisions on this lie any longer. I am not stupid.

To finish the process, you need to replace the lie with the truth. If you don't know what to replace it with, ask God to reveal what the truth is. The Holy Spirit's job is to lead you into all truth.[50] If you can't figure it out, ask a friend, pastor or spiritual leader to guide you to a passage in the Bible you can apply as your truth. Here's a model to replace it:

Holy Spirit, thank you for showing me Your truth. I receive the truth from you that I am smart and have God's favor over my life.

The above models can be adapted to the specific lie you have identified and the truth you need to replace the lie with.

What you believe about yourself will show forth in the words you say which will determine what your life will look like. Speaking forth truth will bring forth a much fuller, more fulfilling life than one framed from lies and bondage. Dig in, start rooting out those lies, and replace them with all the Father has for you!

Controlling Unhealthy Emotions

To orchestrate a successful makeover, unhealthy emotions need to be controlled. To keep our feelings in the caboose, we use the same 3-step approach but apply it to our emotions. First we become aware of what emotion we are experiencing and evaluate the source to *identify* the voice behind the emotion. Next we *determine* our response, whether we want to cooperate with the emotion or not. Lastly, we *process* the feeling by enjoying or exchanging it.

Once we identify a hindering, offending or out-of-control emotion we want to prevent from breeding destruction, we replace it. Oppose unforgiveness. Refuse to hold grudges. Battle against rage. Repel hate. These emotions negatively influence our human relationships. How do we oppose them?

To deal with a negative emotion like rage, firmly state something like:

*Rage, I recognize you. I feel you rising. I will not cooperate with you any longer. I choose to reject the spirit of **rage**. Instead, Father, I ask you to forgive me for letting anger turn into raging actions. I receive Your forgiveness and ask your Holy Spirit to come. I ask for Your **peace**. Release Your **peace** over my body, soul, and spirit. Fill my mind with **peace**. Fill my emotions with **peace**. I receive Your peace right now in Jesus' name. Thank You, Lord, for Your Spirit of rest.*

If we have partnered with an emotion that led to a sinful action, we need to repent. Repentance is the act of admitting our mistake, confessing it to the Lord, receiving His forgiveness, and changing our thoughts and actions to line up with the way God's kingdom works. Repentance is God's way of restoring us back into right relationship.

Here is another example: We could replace *rage* in the prayer with the emotion *discouragement* and replace *peace* in the prayer with the word *hope*. It might sound like this:

*Discouragement, I recognize you. I feel you rising. I will not cooperate with you. I choose to reject the spirit of **discouragement**. Instead, Holy Spirit, I ask you to release Your **hope** over my body, soul, and spirit. Fill my mind with **hope**. Fill my emotions with **hope**. I receive hope right now from the Holy Spirit. Thank you, Lord, for Your Spirit of rest.*

In similar fashion, we can replace depression with joy, self-hatred with love, envy with thankfulness, lust with purity, unforgiveness with forgiveness, selfishness with generosity, revenge with justice, judgment with mercy, bitterness with blessing, disrespect with honor, strife with unity, and so on. For more examples on this concept, I highly recommend Dawna DeSilva's *Shifting Atmospheres*.[51]

Pressing toward Freedom

We obtain freedom from the downward pull of negative emotions if we shift our thinking, change the atmosphere around us through declarations, and follow through with corresponding actions.

Many well-known people mastered their emotions in the midst of unbeatable odds. Imagine how Jackie Robinson's emotions could have screamed for retaliation after the vile expressions of racism he experienced as he became the first black man to play in the National Baseball League. Jackie understood the importance of his opportunity and what was required of him as he blazed the trail for future generations. This enabled him, in the worst pressure cooker imaginable, to consciously control his emotions and behavior under unjust persecution and continue playing baseball to break the cultural barrier wide open.

How do we win during the power struggles we face? Courage. It takes guts to face our past memories and mistakes, root out the lies we have been believing about ourselves and others, and leave the past behind. Once we can take control of the battlefield of the mind, we have completed the main component of the sixth phase of transformation. As we persist in the power struggle, we resist the forces of darkness while God's love leads us in the right direction.

Every makeover has battles to fight and win. To win the power struggle over sabotaging thoughts or negative emotions, we practice self-discipline and self-control to keep our spirit man in charge of our soul. The kingdom of God has everything we need to defeat our nemesis and operate from a new paradigm. Now that we know how to win the power struggle, let's move on to developing our new game plan under the guidance of the Holy Spirit.

A GAME PLAN

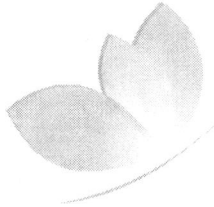

"The game plan worked!" As Lynn lay across the bed exhausted, her voice dripped with satisfaction, "Today was the perfect Disney day." She glanced at her preteen. "I'm so glad I did my research online ahead of time. Did you see those crowds?"

Fidgeting with her phone, Kaitlyn agreed, "Being one of the first people to walk into the park was so cool. We got to go on our favorite rides more than once because we had a game plan of where to start. Those lines could have been a disaster."

Reviewing pictures on her phone, Lynn confessed, "I never knew passing by the rides near the entrance and turning left instead of right could work so well." She handed the phone to Kaitlyn. "It kept us away from the mob so we could get the most out of our day."

"Wow, these are great pics. I'm gonna post some online."

"While you do that, I'm going to see if I can find where I put our game plan for tomorrow," said Lynn with a smile.

≋

To jumpstart our incredible life makeover, a precise, carefully-planned strategy will help eliminate excuses and empower us to take action toward our goals. In phase seven, we develop a kingdom game plan. To sculpt a successful makeover, we need to pick our kingdom, know our kingdom, and defend our kingdom.

Picking Our Kingdom

We have two kingdoms to choose from: the kingdom of darkness and the kingdom of light. The logical choice would be to choose the kingdom of light; however, many people live their entire lives under the dominion of darkness because it seems like too much work to change. Every person has to fight against their lazy flesh. Some people would rather live in chaos than take the time and effort to create order. Everyone experiences pain, confusion, and hard times; it is our personal response that determines what the outcome will look like for us.

Joshua issued a charge to the nation of Israel, "Choose this day whom you will serve; but as for me and my house, we will serve the Lord."[52] In our minds we choose whom we will serve by the thoughts we choose to dwell on. We are encouraged to guard our hearts and minds, for out of them flow all of the issues of our lives.[53] We, as free men and women, have the privilege of choosing to agree with thoughts that agree with the truth of the Lord or the lies of the devil. We have the right and responsibility to choose.

Knowing Our Kingdom

While we were raising our children, we hosted a Brazilian exchange student. After making him feel at home, we scheduled our first family meeting to go over the house rules. We talked about what we expected from him as part of our family and asked him what he needed from us. As a group, we worked together to establish mutual rules which would govern our family, our *kingdom*.

Kingdom Principles

After we pick God's kingdom, we need to understand how it operates. God's ways of operating are different from the world's ways. In fact, the kingdom of light is in conflict with the kingdom of darkness. The principles we live by will govern our behavior and shape our destiny. The powerful truths of the kingdom of heaven may seem foolish to mankind, but as we choose to obey and live according to these truths, we discover they lead to life and freedom.

Here are four examples of opposing kingdom principles.

Kingdom of Heaven	World
To be great in the kingdom, we become a servant.[54]	To be great in the world, we walk over our coworkers and enemies.
In God's way of operating, we overcome evil with good.[55]	When someone hurts us in the world, we get back at them as soon as possible.
In God's economy, it is more blessed to give than to receive.[56]	To make money in the world, we lie, cheat, and steal if we need to.
If we seek the kingdom of God as our first priority, then everything we need shall be added unto us.[57]	If we focus all our time and energy on making money, we will succeed and have everything we need.

In order to operate in the Kingdom of Heaven and receive our kingdom benefits, we need to live like Jesus and follow His advice, "In order to save your life for eternity, you lose your temporal life here on the earth for the sake of the kingdom."[58]

Eternal principles are based on the nature of God. God's nature is loving, merciful, faithful, just, truthful, pure, eternal, and operates in perfect unity and control. The fruit of the Holy Spirit is love, joy, peace, patience, kindness, goodness, faithfulness, gentleness, and self-control.[59] Because the Holy Spirit is inside every believer, we can ask Him to help us live out any of His fruit listed above. Once we understand God is the source of all good, we can study His nature which is expressed through His principles. His nature is the model for our conduct. We want our behavior to be governed by these principles so the fruit of our lives resembles the fruit of Jesus' life.

We start by selecting a characteristic of God that most closely applies to our situation. Let's look at an example of whether or not to cheat on an exam. In this case, we could easily look in the Bible and find that God is the source of all truth.[60] Next we ask ourselves, "What principle of living expresses His truthful nature?"

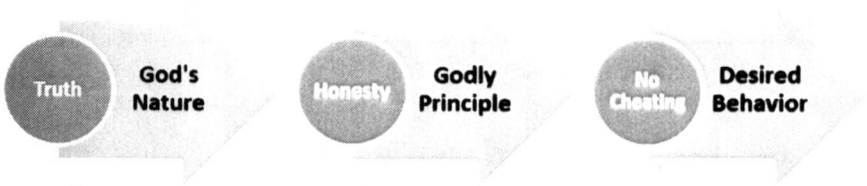

| Truth | God's Nature | Honesty | Godly Principle | No Cheating | Desired Behavior |

Truth leads to good choices.
Good choices lead to receiving the kingdom benefits of:

- Clean conscience
- Inner accomplishment
- Respected reputation
- God's favor

The principle of honesty expresses truth. When we are honest we are aligning with God's nature and His image. If we choose to cheat, we are not being honest about what we know; therefore, we are not telling the truth and not in right alignment with God's nature.

Kingdom Benefits Versus Worldly Results

Timeless standards bring good fruit always because they are based on the character of God. Honesty will always bring us the right result because it is in line with what Jesus would do. A failing student might say, "But to pass the exam, I need to cheat." The student's choice will directly affect his behavior. The same is true for our lives. The kingdom we align our choices with determines whether we reap the benefits of good character or the consequences of poor character.

By choosing honesty, we possess a clear conscience when we leave the classroom. Not only will academic honesty produce an inner sense of accomplishment, but it will also develop a reputation of being honest. The shame of cheating will have an effect that doesn't just disappear after we hand in our test. Even if we don't get caught, we will subconsciously label ourselves as a cheater. If we are found out, we will suffer the academic consequences and possible public disgrace. This makes it simple to see why it is wrong to lie or cheat on any test for any reason.

Every time we choose to operate in alignment with God's character and standards, we make the right choice. This same logic can be followed for every guiding principle of our lives. Once we identify eternal principles that are true for all people at all times in all cultures, we can tie our lifeline to these faith anchors. These anchors empower us to stay stable even during times of stress.

Faith Anchors

Here are four of my faith anchors fixed firmly in my heart.

- God is good all the time.
- God is the eternal source of truth.
- God is always loving.
- God is just.

Like anchors on a ship, faith anchors do not change, no matter what the outward circumstances, and hold us in place during the storms of life. If we give them priority and keep our negative emotions at bay, faith anchors guide our hearts in making wise decisions. What we let into our heart radically influences our lives through our thoughts, words, actions, and habits. In order to protect the condition and content of our hearts, we guard against having contact with any deceitful source and every corrupting influence we can detect.

Are you attached to the wrong anchors?

Whether it is in a physical or spiritual environment, staying attached to the wrong authority produces unpleasant fruit. For example, being a participating member in gang violence usually leads to a great level of personal destruction because gangs are anchored in brutality and bloodshed. Staying entangled with an illegal source of income, which is anchored in dishonesty, breeds nasty consequences like tax fraud and lawsuits. Even if such an entanglement is never uncovered, it hurts the conscience, hardens the heart, and ensnares the participant.

While we are working on our faith walk, our progress can be stopped if we are committed to the wrong authority as a result of clinging to the wrong anchors. Here are some destructive anchors to avoid: God is sometimes good and sometimes bad; God only loves some people; I can't trust God; I am alone. If we are believing any of these destructive anchors, our makeover depends on removing them. We exchange our wrong anchors for faith anchors.

The truth we believe and build our lives on needs to be firmly fixed on the Lord or it will falter under the lies and strategies of the devil. Many people do not want to acknowledge the devil is their enemy; they are more comfortable ignoring him or pretending he doesn't exist. Keeping our head in the sand allows our enemy to continually attack us because our defenses are down. Satan naturally speaks in falsehoods because he is the father of lies; there is no truth in him.[61] Unless his falsehoods are exposed and cast aside, they cause us to doubt God's nature. If we are not careful, we allow error to come in and run rampant. In order to limit their destructive power, reject thoughts that cause division, cast blame, and destroy identity.

The Holy Spirit guides and counsels us daily. If we stay attached to the right faith anchors based on kingdom principles and pursue God's ways of operating, we will enjoy a positive mindset, make better choices, and live in freedom.

Defending Our Kingdom

Because we were created by God with self-rule and given a command to take dominion, God expects us to use our influence for good. There is no profit in having authority if we never exercise it. It doesn't matter if we know what to do if we don't do it. Positive results require action. It is insane to keep doing nothing and expect things to magically change on their own. Wishing things were different or hoping someone else will fix things for us will not alter our circumstances.

Even if we don't have all the details, we can move forward by taking a risk and acting according to what we do know. God can direct our steps if we are moving. A lack of experience is not a valid reason to avoid making a timely decision. Since we can't predict the future with one-hundred-percent certainty, we pray, determine a direction, make an educated decision, and start moving forward.

Overcome Excuses

Sometimes we aren't limited by what we don't know; sometimes we are limited by what we mistakenly think is true. We can easily be deceived into anchoring our lives to excuses. We use all different kinds of rationalizations: I don't have the money to pursue my dreams; I don't have the skills I need; no one will help or support me; I have to quit my job to pursue what I really love to do.

Believing in the mirage of our excuses, instead of God's truth, can make our dreams seem out of reach. We get stuck living small, unsatisfying lives. Excuses thrive when we look at what we don't have and what we can't do. Through sacrifice and determination, we can take steps in a new direction. As we make use of what is accessible, we generate forward progress toward our goals and dreams.

Speak What You Believe

One of the most powerful principles of effective repositioning triggers when you purposefully open your mouth and speak. "I have believed, and therefore I have spoken," communicates this powerfully and simply.[62] Do you speak what you believe or what you think others want to hear? Use the influence of your words to exert your godly will.

Our words contain power; life and death are in the power of the tongue.[63] As we declare words, we plant seeds of either the kingdom of darkness or the kingdom of light. Be careful: what we choose to say today springs forth in our lives tomorrow. Blessings or curses are imparted into lives through our words. Our everyday environment and the surrounding atmosphere are affected by the words we decide to utter.

Act On What You Know

Here is another key that determines our level of progress:

Knowledge acted upon brings results![64]

Even before David was a king, he was a man of action. When David observed Goliath taunting the army of Israel, he asked, "Who is this uncircumcised Philistine that he should defy the armies of the living God?"[65] Can you hear David's confidence in the power and authority available to him as one of God's servants? David's convictions were cemented through personal victories as a shepherd boy when he had killed a lion and a bear. After David's understanding and trust in God developed while out protecting sheep in his private life, he was ready to handle power and authority in a public role. Just like David, we gain knowledge from each victory to use in our next battle.

Conquer Fear

Facing our fears can be as imposing as scaling the north face of Mount Everest. Some people fear losing so they never start. Others are terrified of success because of the attention and responsibility victory would bring. The fear of criticism from someone we admire can cause timidity. Instead of allowing fear to obstruct our future growth, faith empowers us to take steps to move forward, onward, and upward.

Fear is a huge enemy of forward movement. It can be difficult to take lost ground back again. Like David confronting Goliath, we have to stare fear in the face and ask ourselves, "What am I afraid of?" Franklin D. Roosevelt said it best, "We have nothing to fear but fear itself."[66] To evade painful answers, we avoid asking the question. God does not give us a spirit of fear, but instead He gives us a spirit of power, love, and a sound mind.[67] He never intends for us to be ruled by fear. In fact, the opposite is true: our Commander-in-Chief has armed us to overcome fear.

Exert Authority

Proper authority exists when there is power to back it up. Without the muscle to enforce commands, authority is useless.[68] Most of us understand why we need to respect and comply with common authority figures like our parents or the police. Under healthy circumstances, they exert authority over our lives for our benefit. As individuals, we exert power, authority, and control over our lives by our personal decisions.

When a policeman is directing traffic, why do the drivers obey his whistle and hand signals? The traffic cop has authority, delegated to him by the city, which is supported by the *power* necessary to enforce it. When a crisis or crime arises, the police officer has the approval to use force to administer justice and keep the peace. If law enforcement officers didn't have a radio, billy club, and gun, many people would be speeding excessively and robbing convenience stores whenever they felt like it.

Proper boundaries are established and enforced through delegated authority with the will and power to back it up.

We cannot allow a disempowered mindset to deprive us of our power, authority or influence, which reduces our chances for a successful makeover. A victim-oriented, oppressed pattern of thought traps us in apathy and inactivity, rendering us weak and ineffective. Instead of remaining passive, we exert our power, authority, and influence that come from Christ.

To establish new boundaries, we cast aside ineffective reactions, resist foolish temptations, and take action based on God's wisdom. As we develop our analysis and response skills, we can learn to overcome our past conduct. Similar to how learning to ride a bike brings a few bumps, bruises, and skinned knees, improvement is expected if we keep working at it. The goal is progress, not perfection right out of the gate.

Overcome Passivity

When we experience hardship, injustice or other negative conditions, doing nothing often results in a downward spiral of living without purpose. It is easy with 24-hour reality TV, unending movies, and alluring video games to be lulled into a couch-potato mentality and accomplish nothing. Days slip by unnoticed without us producing anything while we are constantly consuming resources. We waste time we can never recoup.

"What do I want? What about me? What do I need?" becomes a circular mantra. I have fallen into this well-camouflaged trap myself and wasted months working on nothing significant.

Imagine a traffic cop sitting all day in the coffee shop, reading the paper, and then going back home. Besides wasting his delegated power and authority due to inactivity, the policeman would not be fulfilling his role in the city either. The public would be paying for services they never received.

You don't have to live under the dominion of the kingdom of darkness any longer. Pick a new kingdom. Open your eyes to the spiritual battle going on around you. In order to put the past behind you, kick the devil out of your territory. Stand and take your position! Forcibly evict the destructive seducer out of your thoughts, emotions, and behavior. Take control and do what you were created to do!

Engaging to Change

Between every decision and the fruit of change is a period of engagement. We engage by putting our thoughts, beliefs, and plans into operation and proceeding with wisdom, courage, and determination. It takes an act of our will to make a decision, engage our resources, and enter into combat. We demonstrate what we truly believe by what we do. In order to accomplish our goals, we contribute our time, money, resources, or energy toward our desired end.

A practical example of the importance of engagement is a lawn mower. When the blade of the lawn mower is not engaged to spin and cut, driving over the grass produces no effect. Endlessly talking about what we should do; could do; or would do, if we had the time and resources, is like driving the lawn mower with the blade up. The grass only gets cut when the blade is lowered and in gear. Solutions appear when we stop the endless talking and get to work.

Engagement

Are we actively engaged with our environments or are we driving around with our blades up? By taking steps of faith amidst risky circumstances, we engage our environments for change.

*Apply influence and personal power to change
your circumstances.*

Our lives improve as we actively engage in living out the principles of the kingdom. The power of darkness tries to replace those principles with lies and half-truths. After we assess what areas of our lives differ with what the Word says about us, we declare truths that correspond with scripture; they always accomplish something.[69] We gain ground as we act upon our declarations.

Influence

A friend of mine mixed the principles of engagement, authority, and influence to change her work environment. As a shift supervisor, she realized she was insulted and offended when coworkers disrespected her or sabotaged the department's production. In order to bring the higher kingdom principle of grace into her work life, she decided to do two things: 1) Respond in an attitude of humility instead of offense and 2) Invite co-workers to treat each other with honor and respect. Her goal was to authentically live out her faith at work and offer the opportunity to others to experience the Kingdom of God.

I asked her, "How did you start this process?"

She replied, "I decided to work for God's approval only and respond in love. Refusing to walk around offended was the key to change the work culture."

I was impressed she took a huge risk to engage her co-workers to share the kingdom in a secular work environment. I couldn't help saying, "Tell me your story."

She modeled her new approach to work stress and strain as the opportunity presented itself. When she responded incorrectly because she was offended, she asked her co-workers for forgiveness, even though it was humbling and hard to do. Relationships began to improve. Some coworkers approached her for advice when they realized they were acting inappropriately because they felt insulted and upset. She explained that forgiving and praying for the other person kept offense out of one's own heart. Those who tried it usually came back later agreeing that praying for the person and the situation made a difference.

There were three clear, positive results from her choice to change her own responses and engage her work culture by using her position of influence and authority for good:

1. She became a happier person and a better supervisor.
2. Several team members learned to extend grace to each other.
3. Their attitude and teamwork improved which also increased their department's productivity.

Reaching Out

We are not alone in this battle to take action. Reach out: God's help is only a prayer away. A father approached Jesus on his son's behalf; the boy could not speak and endured seizures.[70] We can echo this man's cry to Jesus, "Lord, I believe; help my unbelief."[71]

As we begin to walk out our new way of living, God meets us in the small things. We learn as we progress from small victories to larger ones. Our level of cooperation with God determines our integrity and behavior, which shapes destiny.

Allegiance

Allegiance is a powerful word which embodies loyalty combined with commitment and faith. We see this lived out in historical figures such as King Arthur and the Knights of the Roundtable. One of the most notable and praiseworthy qualities of a knight's life is his ability to maintain his allegiance to the king even when facing death. It is not only noble, but a necessary quality that governs the motivation and deeds of the knight. Allegiance to God's kingdom and truth provides a stabilizing foundation on which to build an honorable life with an eternal perspective.

In my own life, I express my loyalty to God by not letting other things like food or sugar addiction, wrong attitudes, possessions, or entertainment crowd God out. Every day I decide whether I will respect and care for people like Jesus or use them for my own purposes. I choose daily whether to worship in the holy of holies with the Holy Spirit or to worship at Hollywood's table. Allegiance is about who we consistently live for and the values we express.

While Satan wants to steal our devotion, God is the One who deserves our worship and allegiance. We can be lured into transferring our loyalty to the wrong authority. Before making new important commitments, let us first examine the character of the person or principles of the organization. We can save ourselves grief and regret later if we will carefully consider if they exhibit the qualities we want to be loyal to. How we allocate our time is how we spend our lives. How and where we spend our time and money testifies to others who and what we are loyal to.

If our habits or actions cause chaos in our lives, we can ponder these questions:

- Am I engaged in defending my territory?
- What allegiances or anchors am I attached to?
- Do any of my allegiances need to change?
- Am I anchored to things that are secure and unchanging?

Exerting Influence

With the gift of free will, we have the opportunity along with the responsibility to exert our influence to overcome challenges to our faith and purpose. Many accomplished people, like Dr. Ben Carson, featured in *Gifted Hands*,[72] overcame imposing odds by intelligently responding to unfair circumstances and staying committed to their unwavering foundational principles. In the movie *Braveheart*,[73] William Wallace remained loyal to his allegiances to family and country and courageously led the battle for Scotland's freedom while facing almost certain death.

Learning to be faithful to the kingdom of heaven is a process. In a kingdom, there is one king and one authority to answer to. Servants of a kingdom, like ambassadors, enjoy the benefits of citizenship. As citizens of Jesus' kingdom, we have a responsibility to joyfully serve our King and then get to enjoy the benefits of the kingdom of heaven. When a kingdom is under siege, the army engages the opposing forces.

The seventh and final phase of transformation is complete when we are equipped and able to execute our game plan. We reach maturity by defending our interests, attacking when we are under siege, and taking back our territory.

Be bold enough to find and use your voice. *Be brave* enough to listen to and follow your heart. *Be strong* enough to participate in the process of change. Follow the game plan!

PART II
LIVING IN FREEDOM

PASS THE TEST

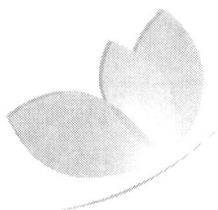

"I am falling out of love with you. I want out. . . ." The words echoed in my head. My heart pounded violently; I felt faint. I could hear myself begging. *I was reduced to begging.* My jumbled words fell on deaf ears. My ex-husband shattered my world. Fear, insecurity, shame, and panic coursed through my body. I trembled violently as I tried to figure out who to call first. I couldn't breathe. I leaned on the counter, dreading what lay ahead.

The human experience is filled with tests, some big, some small. If we live long enough, many of us will go through what I call *the ultimate test*. These severe tests can crush us if we don't have a game plan for staying above the destruction. The biblical strategies embedded within each of the seven phases of transformation provide the stability and support we need to successfully navigate the trials we go through, even the big guns like the top ten stressors.

An ultimate test can be defined as a painful, debilitating loss that threatens to derail us and steal the joy of living. This could come in the form of a major loss such as experiencing extreme mental or physical abuse, divorce or separation, the death of a child or spouse, an addiction, long-term unemployment, imprisonment, or a serious health condition of a loved one or yourself. All major, stressful life events are considered to be in the category of an ultimate test.

When we face an ultimate test, it is important to avoid blaming God for the decisions of other people or for accidents that result from living in a sinful, chaotic world. If we hold God responsible, we may separate ourselves from the source of our strength and recovery. An intimate relationship with God and a connection with friends and family gives us the support and comfort we need to make it through the journey.

When an ultimate test comes, our faith, identity, and confidence go through the fire. By its very nature, fire consumes something for fuel and burns oxygen. The blaze ignited by the distress caused by a major life stressor can put us in jeopardy. If we stay properly connected to the Lord during our trial, He enables us to be purified by the fire without being destroyed. As we pass through a season of suffering, we develop a deeper trust in Him, an appreciation of His nature, and a maturing of our faith.

The opening paragraph of this chapter describes the onset of my ultimate test. To process my grief, pain, and loss, I battled to keep myself in connection with God's presence. I poured my heart out to the Lord; I cried before him in agony. The same Jesus that brought love into my seventeen-year-old heart brought timeless comfort and peace into my shattered adult heart. As I faced the searing pain, I kept breathing and deliberately put one foot in front of the other with the intent to survive.

Since we were both independent agents, created with a God-given free will, I had to respect my ex-husband's choices. He rejected Christ to pursue a different way of living; I could not follow where he was going. We were no longer compatible. He removed himself as my soul mate; I could no longer say, "Good morning, Love."

While I knew I wasn't perfect, my heart broke when I realized I could no longer serve or complete him. He wanted out to spend his future with someone younger.

How did I battle through the loss of my soul mate of twenty-eight years without being destroyed? I survived and passed the test with God's help. He gave me five battle cries.

While going through the inferno of an ultimate test, we need powerful, guiding principles, included in each of the five Battle Cries, for our faith, identity, and confidence to stay strong. The goal of each Battle Cry is to deprive the raging fire of oxygen and fuel so it will not consume us.

Battle Cry 1

With God's help, I will control my thoughts and words;
I will not accept a victim mentality.

Battle Cry 1 gave me fortitude to keep going forward, to force myself to complete hard tasks, and to accomplish small worthwhile projects. I labored daily to reject the bitterness that threatened to overwhelm me. As surges of self-pity washed over me, I fought to keep my head above the powerful waves of depression.

While walking one day, I began by praying again, "I forgive my ex-husband for destroying my life."

The Lord brought me up short by replying, *No, he isn't destroying your life. He is destroying his life as you knew it; only you can destroy your life.*

I abruptly stopped and stood there dumbfounded. In that moment, I was caught up in a huge paradigm shift. My Father in heaven was right; I needed to change my thinking.

Remember: only you can destroy your life.

It was my goal from the start to reject all bitterness and walk in forgiveness, but a sly lie had slipped in. Even though I rejected the label of victim, I felt like one. After twenty-eight years, my husband had changed his mind about his faith, broken his marriage vows, and ended the relationship I had treasured above all others. His actions changed the definition of our family forever. There would be no united legacy. I had to accept his choices and change my thinking.

A large part of my identity and purpose were ripped away by another's decision. While I could not prevent all of the resulting damage, I could control my response. By using self-control, I could still choose how I would think, what I would let pass through my lips, and what I would contribute to the world.

I faced a choice of what I would confess each day. Fueled by agony, anguish, and heartache, voices screamed all sorts of negative junk inside my head. Skills I had developed during my previous makeovers began to override the depressing voices. Within me, the thoughts, *I will not respond as a victim; I am still an overcomer!* rang louder.

To reconstruct my identity, I reinforced my point of view: I was not a victim and I refused to ever live as victim. To take responsibility for limiting the destructive power this loss would be able to inflict on my life, I started to confess:

- Only I can destroy my life, no excuses.
- I will not give up on my God-given identity and calling.
- I will not surrender my rights and inheritance as a daughter of the Most High.
- I will not act or think like a victim; I am an overcomer.

When facing any major stressor, it is important to allow ourselves to feel the pain of mourning. As advised in Lamaze classes regarding childbirth, we have to embrace the pain and work with it. In our minds, we have to face reality and keep moving in spite of the hurt, knowing that getting through an ultimate test won't be easy or quick. When we have a strategy, such as these five battle cries, to keep our thoughts in line, our daily living can remain stable under fire.

Battle Cry 2

With God's help, I will control my response to the pain and trauma; I will not let this loss rob anything else from me.

Titanic, unexpected losses can blindside us. No matter what the damage, we need to control the battlefield of our mind or the effects of the loss will expand. For example, losing a home due to bankruptcy is devastating; if we deal with this event badly, it could spread and impact important relationships, our job, or our health. Dealing with forfeiture poorly can turn a tidal wave into a tsunami. To prevent the storm resulting from our ultimate test from expanding into a level six hurricane, we need to maintain the other areas of our lives, while limiting the effects of the initial hit as much as possible.

In my case, I resolved that even though I had lost my most precious valued relationship, I was not going to surrender anything else that could be preserved by my choices. To the best of my ability, I determined I would not destroy my children, my other relationships, or my future with unwise, destructive choices.

Recovery from any type of major loss is similar to the process of rehabilitation from a severe injury. In my late twenties, one of my lumbar discs bulged and slammed into my spinal cord. Following a week of soaking sheets with sweat and using a bed pan, I was hospitalized for three days and given intravenous pain medication. After six weeks of total bed rest, the pain and inflammation went down. Praise God for chairs with wheels. My first trip shuffling to the mail box seemed like a marathon. During my second lap in the YMCA pool, I thought, *I might drown.* Years later, I was fully recovered.

It can feel the same way in recovery from spiritual, emotional, relational, physical, financial or social devastation. We can experience damage that makes us feel incapacitated. We aren't, but we have to discover how to make our arms and legs work again. Recuperation takes time, but it can be done.

Emotionally we may feel compromised and unsure of how to respond to others.

When emerging from the cocoon I created after separating from my ex-husband, I remember reaching out my hand to greet a man and recoiling in self-doubt. I felt like a duck out of water in an unwanted role as a single person. I avoided direct eye contact with men, trying to contain and mask my trauma. While bandaging my wounds, I learned to function by purposely pushing past my discomfort of reengaging with people.

Step Out of the Shackles

After about two and half months of weeping multiple times a day, the Lord lovingly nudged me along in the letting-go process. In the gentlest voice possible, my heavenly Father told me the shackles had to come off. My heart rebelled, "No, I want to stay in them; I was faithful! I can't imagine life without him." In my spirit, I knew I had to set myself free. To stay mentally and emotionally bound to our marriage covenant, to something that was now dead, would keep me in shackles so I could not move. I could not remain bound to the lifeless carcass any longer.

To step out of the shackles, I also had to let go of my former dreams which included my ex-husband. By cutting my soul tie to him and my ties to everything we had accomplished or planned together, I was able to separate myself from the destruction and distance myself from the barrenness. Once I removed my wedding ring, both in the physical and the emotional realms, I was finally able to look forward. The healing multiplied.

I had to step out because my shackles gave power to bitterness, handed control over to depression, and made the pain of my situation more influential than the love, favor, and faithfulness of God.

Taking off the shackles and purposefully shaking off the heavy spirit of trauma is how we move on from life's major losses. If we lose a person through death, it is healthy to eventually separate ourselves from the trauma of our loss, while honoring our loved one's memory. If we have lost our dream home for whatever reason, we move on by letting go and deliberately stepping out from the chains. In time there will be a new dream for a new home. If it is an emotional loss like being purposefully cut off from a family member, the day comes for us to release our desire for their approval. We are wise to release our grip on the past so it does not choke us any longer.

God is all we need.

How do we find the strength to let go and let God help us move on?

Believe in the BIGness of God

The deposit of God within me strengthened me to do tasks I needed to do but felt too weak to do in my own power. I held fast to my belief that God is good and not the author of death and destruction. In the presence of evil and pain caused by humans, I trusted in, clung to, and relied on my Daddy and His never-changing character. My deep well of intimacy with the Father, that I had developed before my ultimate test began, sustained me in my injured state.

By faith I trusted that my God was so BIG that He would bring good out of this, the biggest, darkest nightmare of my entire life. I determined to remain stable and fixed under the shadow of the

Almighty.[74] God would bring order and new life in the midst of the mess *if I believed* and gave Him time to work on my behalf. Even while I felt blackness all around, God's Spirit inside me empowered me to hope and believe His plan would eventually come to pass.

On the practical side, I realized every day would have its own trouble and comfort; I just wanted to keep breathing and keep moving so I could deal with whatever was required. When I felt shaky or unstable, I took a short self-inventory. When I had a distressing day and needed a listening ear, I called people for comfort and encouragement. I chose self-care activities like walking or going to visit a friend when I sensed despair knocking on my door. Sometimes I needed to laugh or focus on something positive for a while. I also looked for things to do for others when I had the time and resources because healing also comes from the act of giving.

Do you have shackles holding you back? Is what you are focusing on restraining you? Are you ready to let go of what isn't working and start acting on what will bring you freedom and soul peace?

Take Off the Shackles

It is time to surrender and come home to Papa God's love and provision. Believe in His BIGness.

Resist the spirit of trauma and numbness. Trauma causes an instinctive recoiling and turning inward to protect ourselves. Loss can cause us to retract from the world to tend to our wounds. This is a natural, normal human response. Self-protection becomes a problem when nursing our wounds becomes all we focus on every day. The longer we submit to the trauma, pain, and numbness, the tighter and stronger hold they have over us. The prison walls, reinforced by trauma and loss, will confine and control us if we let them.

Resist and reject the continual numbing spirit
that trauma and loss bring.

While nursing my wounds, I decided to live and not die a slow, pitiful death. I resolved to take those things I had previously started and complete them. Finishing this book is an example of how I chose not to let my loss rob anything else from me. I made special appointments with friends to continue searching out manuscript feedback. I enrolled in a writing class. I studied books written by other authors on similar topics.

Managing pain and trauma is difficult, but possible with God's help. He brings us comfort in our time of need and strength to persevere. In due time, freedom is gained by stepping out of the shackles and resisting the cloak of numbing trauma. After the ultimate test comes a new beginning.

Battle Cry 3

*With God's help, I will choose to forgive no matter
how hard it is or how long it takes;
I will not let this loss change me into a self-absorbed,
bitter, angry person.*

Extreme levels of loss tempt us to be bitter, angry people. When we can't find an outlet for our emotions and don't know how to take control over them, they can become our slave driver. When negative emotions overtake us, they can cause us to project a false identity while our true personhood goes into a coma or morphs into a wounded clone. Especially after being blindsided, choosing forgiveness is a key component to ensure self-pity, anger, and bitterness do not become the ruling or corrupting powers over our lives.

God's love is so vast and so brilliant. We hear the love of Jesus expressed as he is dying on the cross: "Father, forgive them: they don't understand what they are doing."[75] He did not focus on His own desires, abandonment, or physical suffering but on the hurting people He was trying to reach. While dying during his stoning,

Stephen said, "Lord, forgive them for this sin."[76] By being Spirit-led, Stephen communicated grace, unconditional forgiveness, and love instead of focusing on his own suffering. Both Jesus and Stephen were expressing the vast, brilliant love God had deposited on the inside of them.

Reconcile with God; forgive yourself and others.

Some people say we don't have to forgive God because He never does anything wrong. They are correct. Sometimes in the agony of life-shattering losses, however, we blame God for our loss or situation because we don't know where else to put the blame. If we become offended by our Father because we think He is the cause of our test or He allowed our loss, we may wallow in the depression pit by believing our pain is His fault. To get out of the pit, we need to reconcile with God as soon as possible by asking God to forgive us and calling on Him to help us recover. Carrying offense or harboring unforgiveness toward our heavenly Father is foolish; by joining with Him He can bring healing and complete restoration.

When we can finally understand God isn't the source of the problem and isn't our attacker, we can stop assigning the blame to God and start properly addressing our pain and grief. When we let go of our perceived right to take revenge for a perceived wrong, we can complete the grief cycle and move on.

Even if it seems impossible to forgive the person responsible for the biggest loss of our lives, forgiveness is non-negotiable. After the ultimate test hits, we recoil; we may be overcome with emotion and respond. But in the end, we forgive others, regardless of their guilt, for our sakes. Jesus forgave in the midst of the most painful death in history. Historians wrote His body was unrecognizable. Stephen forgave as his accusers were stoning him to death.

If we don't know how to cope with the anguish of our ultimate test, we may slip into a dangerous condition resembling an emotional coma. Even in the crucible of a mortal wounding, forgiveness pierces through the darkness to let the process of healing begin.

Forgiveness accelerates the healing process.
Unforgiveness digs a deeper and deeper pit.

True forgiveness is greatness displayed as mercy, whether it be for lies repeated, possessions stolen, identities crippled or marriages destroyed. When we rise above the loss or offense by displaying the kingdom of heaven, the Father's love is revealed on earth as it is in heaven.[77] Forgiveness displays the Father's nature and glory and frees us to move on.

Battle Cry 4

With God's help, I will lean on God and
spend time with my family and friends;
I will not let isolation or depression dominate me.

When we go through a crushing loss and feel like crawling into a hole and disappearing, we find out who our true friends are. We experience how important our connections to the outside world truly are.

I felt like a soldier who stepped on a land mine and
woke up to a body with an arm and a leg missing.

After my ex-husband walked out, it was the small things that equipped me to face the day, one hour at a time. As I faced the trauma, I felt scarred and out of place. The first morning after entering my ultimate test, I trembled as I walked to the kitchen in shock, feeling an undertone of panic. A text arrived from my brother, "Keep your head held high." From miles away, his encouragement caused my shoulders and chin to climb a little higher. My eyes lifted as I whispered to myself, "You can do it. Head high. Don't give in."

Days later, I was still in a cloud of confusion from my ultimate test when I received a text from a friend that dragged me away from a black hole of despair. Hope covered me as my friend wrote, "Just wanted to say how brave you are. Be well, my friend!" I was so thankful for her friendship and that she cared enough to remind me my life *was not* over. In the coming months, her friendship continued to be like a fresh spring bubbling forth in my world.

As I moved through this trial, my eyes were opened to the struggles of others. I listened to gut-wrenching stories from other survivors and learned from all types of tragedy. I was completely taken aback by the strength they had gained from what they had lived through. It became obvious my trial was not unique; many had walked this unhappy path before.

One summer day I unexpectedly climbed to my first mountain-top where I could see above the thick layer of stratus clouds. While visiting my son and going to a baseball game, I forgot about my loss for a few hours and felt a fragile joy of being alive. Sitting with a warm breeze hitting our faces, we were entertained by multiple home runs and close plays. Even better, our team won. The delight of being with my son washed over me; joy quietly crept in. Time helps the healing process. Give yourself time.

Allow others to invest in your recovery.

The value of family, friends, and coworkers can never be overstated as we try to find our moorings. In our vulnerable state, it can be difficult to accept the acts of kindness that parents, siblings, friends, and coworkers carry out as they observe our struggle. To stay connected during our recovery, we communicate trust by allowing others into our pain, to listen and offer advice. Even if we are not comfortable asking for help, accepting comfort and counsel from others helps us as we journey back toward normal.

As human beings, we have a need for physical touch. Our friends' hugs remind us of how much they care. When we feel crippled and under attack, it is easy to retreat into a shell of pride or fear. Resist the urge to retreat! Wisdom assigns us the task of telling our caretakers how we are doing. Keeping our friends fully informed increases our level of accountability and allows them to lighten the weight of our burden. While some people may disappoint or ignore us, those who truly care will surprise us as they shed light into our darkness.

When one candle is used to light another candle, the first candle doesn't lose any light but multiplies the light. By sharing the good times and the bad times, we can help keep each other's candles burning.

Battle Cry 5

*With God's help, I will continue to pursue my dreams and
my destiny; no matter what, I will not let this loss define
my identity or purpose.*

After about three months of intense grieving, I realized my dreams needed to be forged into something radically different. Through prayer, I formulated several positive confessions over myself. I forced myself to say them out loud, even though I didn't always feel like they were true. My feelings were encased in such deep grief and sorrow that I knew keeping my emotions in the caboose during this recovery was vital to my survival. I visited the caboose to grieve, but I didn't stay there all the time.

To combat my feelings of being overwhelmed, naïve, and helpless, I went to sleep to the sounds of worship or my favorite motivational speaker. I intentionally filled my mind with positive thoughts to keep hope alive. Here are some examples of what I meditated on to limit the effects of the loss:

1. While I am grieving, I will depend on God for healing.
2. I will give and receive love from God and people in my safety net.
3. I will continue to be a person of faith, character, and integrity.
4. I will not carry hatred, shame or guilt around.
5. I will not let this loss rob anything else from me.
6. God will use my pain and experience for something really good.
7. I will be a distribution center of the kingdom of God.

While my heart was initially broken into tiny pieces, God not only healed it but filled the void left by my ex-husband. After about seven months of battling this trial, people noticed I was different. They said though I was loving before, I had even more compassion now. Going through this loss increased my capacity to relate to the pain and heartache of others.

No one wants to go through an ultimate test because such major life events change us through a hot, raging fire. However, after our impurities are burned away, we walk in greater clarity, purity, and purpose than we did before.

In the middle of the confusion and struggle, our help comes from God.

Hope and Healing

During my ultimate test, God's love brought hope and healing to me. When I cried or went through an emotionally bloody interchange, I found comfort in the phrase, "The healing has begun." These four little words inspired hope because the life-giving power of God had entered into the situation. This phrase brought me comfort because it signaled there would be an end to my remolding process. If the healing had begun, healing was already in process *and* would have an end.

While I was going through a horrible trial that routinely devastates many women and men, my own manuscript for this book became a source of counsel. The words I had written in previous years reminded me of what to do to preserve my identity and restore my injured soul to wholeness. After a long and difficult transition, I am thankful God healed my broken heart and resurrected my determination to really live. He has given me the courage to share about my wounds, which are a window to my soul, to tell my story to help others.

God's love brings hope and healing into every situation, even when we cannot hear or see Him. The healing love of God surrounds us and makes us whole and complete. The healing forgiveness of God keeps us clean and in a place where we can hear Him speak to us.

Whether in prayer or worship, through a friend's embrace, or by hearing the truth in the Word, the love of God keeps hope alive!

Every day of a makeover, especially during an ultimate test, can be hard work. What is our alternative? Self-pity? Depression? Hatred? These are deep, dark traps Satan tries to pull us into. Our connection to the Source of True Goodness helps us stand instead of being crushed. Our unchanging anchors, the Word of God and the guidance of the Holy Spirit, enable us to rebuild our lives.

Even though each ultimate test is unique, as experienced by an individual, these kingdom principles are universal. If we adapt and apply these battle cries to our particular situation, they will empower us to triumph and overcome adversity.

I encourage you to fight the good fight of faith. Don't look back. Stay the course and run your race with courage. If you are enduring one of life's ultimate tests, I would love to hear your story and how God is bringing you through. I know with perseverance, you will accomplish an incredible life makeover!

BE AUTHENTIC

Fidgeting to find her credit card in the checkout line, Hope's eyes skim the magazine covers, proudly parading the airbrushed faces of the famous, magnifying their imperfections. The sensationalism by The *National Exposer* hits a sore spot, "Anti-anxiety drugs lead to dementia." Repulsed by the hype and advertising, she thinks, *You've got to be kidding. I'm so sick of this. There's got to be more to life than this!*

Taking off her makeup before bed, Hope leans toward the bathroom mirror and sighs, "I can't do this anymore." Staring at her naked face, she searches her soul, "Where do I find peace and satisfaction? My diamonds sparkle. All my clothes are name brand. The new car smell is already gone. Even on vacation with friends, my sense of despair lingers in the background. Where is this elusive happiness? What am I missing?"

The small still voice of the Holy Spirit whispers, "I am here. Nothing is missing. You are looking in the wrong places. Look within to discover who I created you to be. In My love, you are complete. You were created to be amazing and wonderful, just as you are."

Self-Discovery

Arriving at the place where we know who we are takes investigation and trial and error. If we remove our blinders, we can discover who we really are and honestly assess our lives so we don't waste them away. Here are three questions to start the self-discovery process:

1. Who have I been trying to be? (past tense and closed)
2. Who am I now? (present tense and beginning to open)
3. Who do I want to become? (future tense with great potential)

The answers to these three questions spark stimulating debate. It can be helpful to ferret out information about the first question from those who know us best. We can easily fool ourselves into thinking we are one person while we masquerade as another. It is revealing when others express what they have experienced with and observed about us. The differences between their descriptions and our best intentions can be startling.

Learning From Our Past

An effective game plan has a definite starting point and an end goal in mind. A game plan is useless if we won't implement it because of faulty thinking. We may stop moving if we think our flaws or mistakes will be exposed. We will never change if we can't see anything wrong with our past decisions or how we are currently living.

The first steps toward changing a bad habit are to identify it, accept responsibility for our mistakes, confess any sin or mistakes to God, change directions, and then tell someone else for added accountability.

Early in my first makeover as a seventeen year old, God began to lovingly mold me to create a new identity within me. He showed me how my response to pain and heartache had caused a misshapen identity. Even though it was not my intention as a teenager to be inconsiderate, I had a self-centered, victim mentality that oozed self-pity into every encounter. Self-pity drove me to focus on how dreadful my life was. I shifted the blame for the condition of my life squarely onto the shoulders of others. It wasn't my fault – no way! But God had something better for me in mind.

In reality, it was my fault because I chose my response, mindset, words, and actions. Was this easy to admit? No. Did I finally realize I needed to change? Yes. I had reached the point of wanting to enjoy my life and recognized the steps necessary to prevent self-pity from dominating my personality and conduct.

For those needing a makeover in one or more areas, identifying problem areas by honest self-assessment can be heartbreaking, scary, and depressing. In my early thirties as a young mother, I remember bawling my eyes out the day I realized how self-focused, self-righteous, and self-justified I was. I felt sick to my stomach as my insides were ripped away. I identified that selfishness was destroying my life just as alcohol does for the alcoholic. Once I was ready to take responsibility and change, I confessed it to the Lord, my family, and my closest friends. If I had kept my blinders on, I would have missed most of the relational blessings of my life! It was worth every sob and pain-filled decision to realign my motives and actions.

Learning from the past prepares us to be authentic and take ownership of our actions.

Taking Ownership

We choose our responses to what life throws at us. Our decisions impact the fruit we bear. Our choices come with unknown responsibilities and unexpected outcomes we may not fully understand at the moment. If we have obeyed God's Word and guidance, we can be confident we have made the right determination no matter what the outcome.

Experience is life's most talented teacher. Nothing can replace experience because we learn certain critical life lessons only by persisting and working our way through problems. Experience prepares us for elevated vision and maturity to use in building the life God wants for us.

As we plunge into our incredible life makeover, discovering our true selves is important so we don't head off in the wrong direction. In the pursuit of answers, we can be encouraged because we carry the kingdom of God within us.[78] Our authenticity flows from this inner source of identity, value, and purpose.

To help you flush out your authenticity, answer these questions of self-reflection:

Who am I now?
What did I enjoy doing as a child?
What gifts do I possess from Father God?
What experiences do I look forward to?
What character traits do I value most in myself and others?
Who do I want to be?

It would be a tragedy to successfully make over a life into something someone else wants or expects. To avert such a tragedy, answer these questions after some serious soul-searching:

Do I know my divine purpose?
Am I hiding my gifts and talents?
Am I developing my gifts and talents?
What voices do I need to silence?
What challenges do I need to make myself face?

Accepting Ourselves

After going through the process of self-exploration, learning to accept ourselves is next on the agenda.

Living as God's Creations

We are all created from the breath of God with a God-given personality. For years, I didn't like my personality. I wanted to be someone else, anyone else. I kept bumping against the porcupine quills of other porcupines. I thought if I could only be quiet, we wouldn't be stabbing each other. I thought if I talked and explained myself more clearly, we wouldn't be jabbing each other. If only I could be a mind reader or perform to everyone's standard of perfection, we wouldn't be poking each other. None of these solutions worked.

As these fallacies dropped away, I began to accept myself for who I was and how I was created. As a result I was able to lower the pressure on myself and others to perform perfectly. The porcupine-quill poking sessions dwindled and grew less painful. As I began to like myself more, my defensive behaviors softened. I opened previously closed doors and invited others to join me in life's adventure. When I was criticized, I temporarily retreated to safety but soon reemerged to begin again. The connections I was able to re-establish with family and friends was worth all the effort.

As you pursue living the purposeful, enjoyable life you've imagined, live it authentically. Most people want to be in heartfelt relationships with sincere people who admit they have problems. While shallow people might reject you if they see your imperfections, remember the benefits and satisfaction of authentic relationships far outweigh the risks. Just as people want to eat authentic Mexican food, wear authentic designs, and drink "The Real Thing," they want to be in genuine relationship with the true you. We learn to be authentic when we let go of who we "should" be and embrace and live out who we really are.

Living in the Wild

Authentic living during a makeover takes extended effort. Coming out from our cage, we now take our places out in the wild, where we will have to compete for resources to survive. In nature, there are dangerous predators and places of refuge; likewise, we may encounter unfair or tough situations and then find wonderful peace and ease in other circumstances. During the course of change, we keep our eyes on our game plan even while we adapt to those around us and occupy our position.

Authentic living is not going to be a cake walk. Real life sometimes slaps us across the face as we endure disappointments, bitter losses or unfair betrayals. The hardness of life can sidetrack us. How do we develop mental toughness? We restrain ourselves from escaping into online social media or our favorite cell phone game. In order for our makeover to succeed, we raise our level of awareness, take stock of what is going on, and function with common sense mixed with tenacity.

Life may be harder outside the cage, but we were designed to live in the wild and take dominion everywhere the sole of our foot treads.[79] We are meant to run our race and soar like eagles. If we trust God to be our source of strength, we shall run and not be weary; we shall walk and not faint.[80]

Living Authentically

Once we appreciate who we are and understand our purpose, these realizations provide a platform of freedom and stability for us to push off from. If I like riding my bike in the middle of a Wisconsin winter, I am free to do so. If I want to shave my head bald, no one can stop me. If I want to walk across America and raise awareness for breast cancer, I can. I don't have to bungee jump off a bridge to prove myself. When I know my strengths and limitations, I can focus on making progress and using my resources wisely.

Sometimes we catch ourselves focusing on how "lucky" other people are instead of building our own authentic life. It's easy to admire people from afar and imagine their lives are easy and picture-perfect. As we interact with them, however, we discover everybody has problems and seasons that are painful or difficult. Our pain is no different from their pain. Life does not always treat us fairly, but we move forward by holding our head up and keeping our focus on overcoming our challenges.

Living Without Worry

We worry far too much about what other people think. Why? I used a clever phrase with my teenage children during their high school years. As needed, they repeated the phrase out loud:

> *Don't worry about what other people*
> *think of you because they don't.*

I massaged the concept into their minds that their friends were too busy thinking about themselves to be thinking about them.

It is much more productive to think positively and live true to our convictions than living to please other people. This creates a positive energy and the mindset necessary to shift directions. Self-acceptance and a positive approach builds the confidence we need to set a goal and make decisions to move forward.

"Follow your heart" is great advice. We are empowered when we freely express who we are, within reason, rather than who we think others want us to be. If we, as individuals, can honestly look at ourselves in the mirror and say, "I accept myself and am pushing towards my future," we are ready for a breakthrough. In *Hamlet*, William Shakespeare voiced this profoundly and simply: "To thine own self be true."[81]

Turning Points

Restoration and recovery are possible. Growth can happen quickly once we see what change is needed. The day I faced the real me, I was filled with disgust. Hope came to the rescue as I made the following realizations:

I didn't want to be selfish; I wanted to be loving.
I didn't want to be pitiful; I wanted to be powerful.
I didn't want to be negative; I wanted to be positive.
I didn't want to be consumed with fear; I wanted freedom.
I didn't want to be full of pent up anger; I wanted to feel joy.
I didn't want to carry the past anymore; I wanted a better future.

I needed a new paradigm with new goals because I wanted to express the beauty of my Lord and His glorious kingdom. I wanted to express who I was becoming as His daughter. I dedicated my time and energy to allowing the Holy Spirit to transform me from the inside out. I wanted to press toward my future instead of allowing my past to dictate what I could and could not do. Since I desperately wanted a different future, I chose the pain of change.

Choice is a gift we all receive from our Creator; learning to draw from our God-given reservoir of personal power is critical. Once again we hear the echo of Moses, "Choose life, that you and your family may live."[82] During our personal renovation, we should remodel wisely; all of our decisions have consequences, intended and unintended. Many times the wisest option has all of the luscious fruit buried under a hard beginning. For example, peace at the next family gathering may be buried under the pressure of confronting a current family conflict. As you stare at the north face of the mountain, giving God permission to take complete control is the beginning of your new high adventure.

Many times we will choose to endure our current condition UNTIL . . .the pain of changing IS LESS THAN the pain of staying where we are.

It can be painful when we become conscious of the gap between where we are today and where we want to be in the future. If we let the devil keep us in the dark, unaware, and ill-informed, he can keep us sick, miserable, and weak. In order to break out of this condition, we sacrifice in the short term to invest for our long-term advancement. History and personal experience tell us that cooperating with our Father's eternal principles, even though it may be going against the grain, is worth it.[83] Choosing wisely today and going through the pain of change will lead to receiving our inheritance of love, power, joy, and freedom. Who wouldn't want an inheritance like that?

Finding Our Passion

During our transformation, we identify through self-exploration and discovery what is honestly in our heart and makes us tick. This expedition may seem like climbing Mount Everest. Just as reaching the summit brings every climber hard-earned satisfaction, finally unearthing who you are will bring an inner feeling of wholeness money cannot buy.

On the journey of self-discovery, we determine what we want our lives to stand for and how we can proceed accordingly. These are tough questions no one else can answer for us. If we believe in the right to bear arms for self-defense, we should be able to stand and defend our belief. If our focal point is conquering world hunger, we might start a local organization to feed the poor with a vision to expand overseas.

The principles we are willing to promote and support will be part of our legacy imparted to our children and community. Sometimes what we endorse will bring conflict, even with those we care about, but if we do not stand for the principles we believe in, we will not have a lasting, positive impact. Choose guiding principles carefully and make every effort to implement them into daily living. Always strive to preserve relationship and prefer reconciliation.

Your heart intuitively knows what you want to become.

Steve Jobs, founder of Apple Inc., understood how important it is to use time effectively: "Your time is limited, so don't waste it living someone else's life. Don't be trapped by dogma - which is living with the results of other people's thinking. Don't let the noise of other people's opinions drown out your inner voice. Most important, have the courage to follow your heart and intuition. They somehow already know what you truly want to become. Everything else is secondary."[84]

As we learn to challenge our past fears, freely express who we really are, and face the uncertainty of the future with courage, we provide the paint and palette for authentic living.

MANAGE STRESS

"I said, I have everything under control," disagreed Mary, every curt syllable dripped with tension as she placed her earrings on the dresser.

"I think you're taking on too much. Be reasonable," pleaded Steven. "No one can work sixty hours a week, take care of their dying mother, and direct the school musical."

"Of course I can. I have to. I need to," explained Mary. "While he's on vacation, my boss is counting on me to coordinate our top client's merger. I text mom's ICU nurse to check on her during the day. Then, either before or after work, I stop in to see her. Everything is fine, just fine." Mary tossed her shoes toward the pile in the corner and collapsed on the bed.

As he knelt and gripped her quivering shoulders, her husband shook his head. "Honey, you're gonna collapse if you don't get some help. Maybe you should hand off the musical."

"But the kids are counting on it, though they need to take practice more seriously. You know how tight money is. This play has to be a financial success, or the Theatre Guild will go under. I can't let that happen."

"Take some time to think about this. You'll never forgive yourself if you don't take time to be with your mom before it's too late."

"Don't worry. I can handle it," Mary reassured him. Her hands trembled as she lifted the coffee cup to wash down the sleeping pills. "I have to keep going, don't I? There isn't anyone else who can do it." She hesitated. "I just can't face one more loss. Dad's death almost killed me."

Mary isn't coping with her stressors very well. She is stuffing her fear of death, fear of disappointing the Theatre Guild, and fear of failure at work with perfectionism. She could use some healthier coping mechanisms to get through the convergence of these crises. In order to maintain her mental health and emotional well-being, self-care is essential. Carving out time for worship, Bible study, and prayer would be the most important place to start. Mary needs to stay full of the Holy Spirit and truth to remain stable and peaceful. By spending time feeding her spirit man, she will be better equipped to meet the needs of others.

Mary also needs to find practical ways to deal with the pressure. She could ask for a temporary leave of absence from work, call a family member to help with her mother, or hand off the school play to another qualified volunteer. To meet her emotional needs, Mary could start by getting some counseling or spending meaningful one-on-one time with her husband or best friend. By walking outside at a park or laughing at a funny movie, she could relieve her physical stress.

Human beings have built-in defense mechanisms to create distance from the stress of life's major positive changes, negative events, or relational challenges. Correctly used, these mechanisms help us cope with the ordeals, insults, and injuries that come into our daily lives. These mechanisms become a problem, however, when we swing to the extreme and become defensive or evasive in our interactions.

To cope with life's seasons of stress, it is important to see our defense mechanisms in a correct light. While God is our first line of defense, sometimes a healthy level of self-protection is wise and necessary. However, when self-protective coping behaviors are pushed to the extreme, they may hinder your life instead of helping it. Coping mechanisms, when not kept in check, can wall us in and keep us from becoming who we were born to be.

Coping Mechanisms

During a brief visit to any junior high, we would see at least five unhealthy coping mechanisms popping out all over the place. Very few people want to relive being thirteen again due to the painful, confusing transition of passing from the innocence of childhood into the reality of adulthood. Masks camouflage our junior high insecurity, uncertainty, lack of identity or fear of the future. Regardless of our age, we have all worn a mask as we attempted to cope with a stressful situation.

These behaviors have strengths and weaknesses. Problems develop when we use coping mechanisms at an extreme level to mask issues or problems. We will consider the weaknesses of five masks. Unfortunately, the strengths of healthy coping mechanisms become liabilities when they are incorrectly applied or overused.

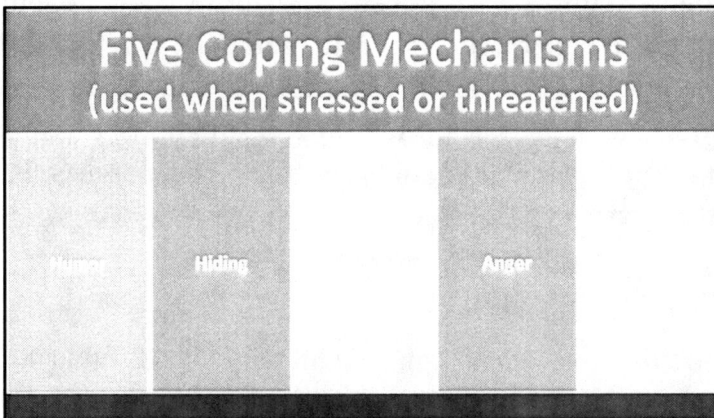

Five Coping Mechanisms
(used when stressed or threatened)

Humor   Hiding   Anger

Hollow Humor

The class clown cracks jokes to lighten the mood when things get too serious. We secretly admire him as he takes the attention off of us and makes us laugh. We think, *I wish I could make people laugh like that.*

God has a sense of humor and loves to hear you laugh. Gaze at His creation—you can see His sense of humor. During an aquatics show, think about how the playful dolphins prompt us to laugh. As children watch Wally the penguin waddle around in the movies, joy and giggles fill the theatre. The antics of baby kittens chasing a ball of string can make anyone smile. God created creatures like the duck-billed platypus because they delighted Him so much!

The Bible says, "A cheerful heart is good medicine, but a crushed spirit dries up the bones."[85] Laughter helps us relieve stress and improves our health and well-being. It isn't healthy to be serious all the time. Ecclesiastes says there is a time to mourn and a time to laugh.[86] Joking and giggling together creates a different kind of connection in our relationships because we are willing to share another side of ourselves. Comedians are gifts to keep us in touch with the humorous, lighter side of life.

When we take laughter, however, and make it into a shield, it can become a screen we hide behind to mask our true feelings. Let laughter cultivate her appetizing fruit in your life, but never use humor to conceal an issue with someone that should be addressed privately with sensitivity. Laughter is a wonderful coping mechanism to help us deal with difficult situations. It is important we do not use it to divert attention from crucial issues that need to be dealt with or discussed.

Hiding in a Fox Hole

In a crowded junior-high lunchroom, we see other excesses. While one young woman talks and talks and talks, or to put it bluntly, never shuts up, another hides in the corner and never talks. Both extremes hurt our development and connectivity; both are forms of hiding.

The excessive talker obscures her insecurity with noise, never letting anyone else in on the conversation. She babbles a million words and never says the one thing her soul is screaming.

The girl hiding in the corner tries to make herself invisible to escape the pressures of talking, so she might hide behind her book, a safe and trustworthy friend. Although books fill her imagination to distract her from her problems, the pages may also stifle her healthy inner voices that are waiting to be heard. If she never speaks, she is hiding in a hollow, empty place.

There are other unhealthy ways of hiding. People conceal their needs and repress their voices in excessive exercise, drugs, alcohol, online gaming, pornography, gambling, and countless other masks. These unhealthy ways of hiding have drastic drawbacks that can totally overtake our recovery, derail our progress, and eclipse our future. By hiding underground, we can conceal ourselves from others; ignore issues that cry out to be dealt with from our past or present; and suppress our pain, our doubts, and our fears.

The problem occurs when some form of hiding is used as a means of escape to protect ourselves from normal levels of risk. To avoid abuse of this coping mechanism, we can purposely remove our superficial mask when we are healed and carefully merge into the ecosystem of life. As we move toward connection and enter into relationships, it can feel awkward and unnerving.

Find your courage to connect and contribute within your sphere of influence.

There are times when hiding is a healthy coping mechanism. When we are under attack, sometimes we withdraw to protect ourselves from harm. If we have experienced a big loss or disappointment, keeping quiet and out of sight can also be healthy to allow us time to process our grief or analyze what we did wrong or how to proceed. Hiding becomes unhealthy when it is pushed too far for too long.

God encourages us to sit in His presence and spend the night in His shadow because He desires to be our refuge in times of trouble, our rescuer from hidden traps, and our shield from deadly hazards.[85] When we reject unhealthy hiding and choose to trust in God instead, we are safe. His huge, outstretched arms and comforting embrace keep us perfectly sheltered from harm. Sitting in God's lap and depending on His protection and provision is the smartest choice we can ever make!

The Idol of Intellectualism

We move on to the proud, arrogant juvenile, reducing his peers to subpar while flaunting his superior algebra test score. He lofts himself higher than the rest of the class by boasting of his expertise and superior intellectual knowledge. From his prominent vantage point, he is safe from their ridicule and mundane social drama. An esteemed quest for knowledge has mutated into a self-absorbed, revolving search for self-importance.

Intellectualism can be a tricky coping mechanism to balance. Our intellectual ability is a gift from God meant to be balanced by a willing heart, positive attitude, and good character. We should develop our gifts, talents, and minds to our full potential. Exploring other options and increasing our storehouse of knowledge can also be a great way of dealing with stress. As a side benefit, life-long learners normally live longer. Instead of giving our minds over to imagining the worst, we can continue to grow by feeding our spiritual and intellectual appetites.

Pride over our accomplishments ought to be kept in check, or conceit will destroy us, gradually dismantle our relationships, and come between us and God. Scholars should not allow their identities to be based solely on their intellectual ability to acquire knowledge as it is only a partial expression of who they are. We guard against any thought that our academic education elevates our status higher than anyone else.

Jesus used His time and energy to seek out the lost, the sick, and the hurting to bring restoration. Jesus selected fishermen, tax collectors, and a political zealot as His disciples; none of them were theologians. In fact He spent so much time with the common folk He was criticized by the Pharisees for eating with crooks and riffraff[88] and labeled "a glutton and a drunkard, a friend of tax collectors and sinners."[89]

While Jesus was superior in every way, His intellectual abilities were united with a servant's heart and an outreaching attitude to touch and transform lives.

When we use our knowledge and skills to better the lives of others instead of competing with them, we look like Jesus. With a thankful attitude for what we have been given, we should develop our minds and watch for opportunities to use our resources to build people up. Our God-given talents, when used to make a positive contribution to society, will make room for us. Humble yourself in the presence of the Lord, and He will lift you up.[90] As we use our gifts to benefit others, we will be elevated and our lives will be made significant.

Dagger of Anger

As our junior-high movie plays on, two adolescent males, full of anger and testosterone, plunge into a scuffle and trade blows and insults in the hallway. Their lack of communication skills combined with the undeniable need to protect their reputations fuels the battle. Rage and violence are used to camouflage their need for guidance and to avoid asking for help to cope with their problems. They must, at all costs, preserve the façade of toughness and supremacy. As they stay mired in inner conflict under the disguise of anger, they are robbed of delightful moments that could later be replayed as treasured memories. If the inner denial continues, it will steal their future dreams. Our prisons are full of men who were wrongfully convinced of the necessity of their masks to hide their individual needs and deepest desires.

When young men and women cope by carrying deep-seated anger, they face a long and lonely road. To hide their hurts and fears, they use anger to cut others off. In their minds, expressing their true feelings to others would communicate weakness and admit defeat. Nothing could be further from the truth. As they struggle to hide their pain, they remain closed vessels filled with infection. Only in uncovering their wounds and dropping their defenses can their injuries be cleansed and healed.

To avoid falling into this trap ourselves, it is important to admit what we need. Instead of using anger as a defense, it is wise to neutralize the dagger of anger in our lives. If inner toxicity is not allowed to drain, it poisons our systems. Sooner or later, unresolved bitterness and resentment causes emotional and physical disease.

Those hiding behind anger are trying to suppress their pain behind concrete walls. However, anger is a symptom of a wrong, real or imagined, which is calling out to be dealt with. Anger dissipates when it is given an acceptable outlet to provide for a controlled release. How we perceive things drastically affects when and how anger shows up.

Anger is an emotion we experience as a result of the fall of man in the Garden of Eden. It can be natural to feel anger when we see sin, injustice, rebellion or wrong attitudes. In this case, anger can highlight a situation needing prayer and further attention. Many times, however, anger is an emotion based in pride that causes us to hurt others with our temper. When we give ourselves over to the control of anger, we sin. The Bible says to "Be angry, and do not sin."[91]

Anger can come from imagined offenses, real injuries or a combination of both. The pressure can be released by addressing the cause or source of the irritation. When we feel anger, it is important to identify the real root of what we are actually angry about.

If someone has hurt us and we are angry, we can take it to the Lord and ask Him what we should do. Sometimes His answer leads to confronting a person or organization's actions. Confronting in love, after we have carefully prepared our hearts for the encounter, can bring about a much better outcome. At other times His direction requires doing nothing outwardly but forgiving and praying for the person or situation. We can trust God to defend us and clear our name if we have acted with integrity and decency.

Forgiveness and reconciliation are better tools than bottling up anger or releasing violence. Love calls us to bear with each other[92] and makes us willing to forgive many sins against us.[93] If we let truth in and the infection out, we can courageously address relationship issues without the hindrance of unhealthy anger.

Shield of Perfectionism

Finally, we shift our focus to the junior high overachiever, driven to achieve perfection in every class, every project, every performance, every sport, and every conversation. Drowning in insecurity, they agonize over exceeding expectations in every area of life hoping to receive the respect, value, and acceptance they crave. They operate under a false sense of reality that external forms of achievement, acknowledgement or affirmation will meet their innermost need of validation. Unfortunately, most recognition lasts for fifteen minutes and then life marches on.

Perfectionism means many things to people. It may be someone's life goal to be perfect for a moment; like scoring a perfect 10 on a vault at the Olympics or winning a Super Bowl. For another person, it may be the joy of playing a Mozart symphony in perfect pitch. Striving toward excellence while pursuing such goals is a good thing if the pursuit makes our heart sing and springs from the right motive. Healthy perfectionism can be described as a focused pursuit of excellence.

Unhealthy perfectionism becomes a cruel shield of control when we believe perfection is the only acceptable result or we are worth nothing. If we are trying to present a picture-perfect façade externally to validate ourselves because internally we are incomplete, defective or insecure, we may easily fall prey to unhealthy demands.

When not kept in balance, perfectionism can create control addicts that drive themselves and others to the breaking point by incessantly cleaning, working, serving, etc. Meticulousness can become a way of life we mistakenly use to manage every aspect of our environment. Unhealthy perfectionism is the self-striving to mask discontentment, self-hatred, insecurity or shame. Unfortunately, the extended stress from the exacting rules and regulations can cause lives to crack, crumble, and break. The intense pressure can crush us inside a steel trap if we try to perform perfectly and expect others to live up to impossible standards.

In stark contrast, it is our relationship with God, inner sense of purpose, and connection to other human beings that brings meaning to our existence. While avoiding the negative trappings of perfectionism, God calls us to "put on love, which is the bond of perfection."[94] His call to holiness is a life-long pursuit to align our lives with God's nature, character, and power. His call is not a plan of earning our right to be good enough to go to heaven, but He calls us out of every damaging trap of the enemy and into a full expression of His love and goodness. This striving is a good, but very challenging, quest for perfection that will only be completed in heaven. Striving for external perfection for approval is harmful and very restricting; wanting a heart that is full of God's love and wanting to give it away is freedom!

Living with Limitations

Individuals applying a coping mechanism in an unhealthy manner need to overcome their desire to conceal their flawed but beautiful self. Whatever coping mechanism we are using to manage stress should be kept in balance. By taking proper care and staying alert, we can avoid pushing the strength of the mechanism too far and distorting the behavior management tool into a weakness.

We, as humans, cannot be what God is.

Consider the fact that only God is perfect and the source of ALL that is good. No human is perfect—no, not one. Instead of trying to live a perfect life according to our will and expectations, we should put ourselves into His loving hands and cooperate with His perfect will on a daily basis. If we have a tendency toward wearing a mask, repeating statements like these out loud daily will tear down the need for disguises and release the faith to walk in freedom:

- I am not God.
- My spirit is perfect in Christ.
- God loves me just the way I am.
- With God's help, I grow and mature daily.
- God does not expect me to perform perfectly.
- I like myself and accept I have strengths and weaknesses.

Confessing these to yourself will free you from your unrealistic expectations or the expectations others may have placed upon you. Do this for thirty days. You will be amazed at how much better you feel.

We are human beings, not human doings.

I have inconvenient shortcomings that become evident on a regular basis; I have labeled them Julie-isms. Whether it is leaving my kitchen cabinet doors open every time I cook dinner or misplacing my keys once again, my flaws are proof I am still alive. Praise God I am not dead and can contribute to make the most of each day.

As three-part beings, we all have limitations. Our weak points can cause us to lean in to the Father's chest and listen for His voice. Our weaknesses can be covered by God's mighty strength and power. The Apostle Paul boasted in his weaknesses so others would be drawn to the demonstration of Christ's power working through him.[95]

By accepting how we are made and the weaknesses that come with it, we step out into the light without using coping mechanisms as a shield. This allows us to connect in a childlike way to God's love and His guidance. It feels a little scary to let people see our warts and scars, but that's okay. It is our humanity showing through which makes us more endearing to people. Allowing for the failings and idiosyncrasies of others can help us accept our strengths and weaknesses. Having an attitude of love and grace toward others and ourselves allows us room to breathe, to come to grips with who we are (and are not), and to search for our place to bloom.

It is hard to find a real pine tree that offers the perfect shape of an artificial tree; but we love the smell and texture of a real Christmas tree. The same is true of our existence; our smell, texture, and imperfections are what make us appealing and approachable.

It can be a messy business to change behavior patterns and adjust our coping mechanisms. As we move toward recovery and relationships develop, it becomes obvious which reactions need to change. As we move toward a healthy middle ground, this transition takes time so we need to be patient with ourselves.

Coping through Relationship

We are each created with a unique design. Each personality uniquely expresses the life force we are born with. Joy in one person might express itself in loud and expressive laughter; joy in another person might burst forth silently like bright sunshine beaming from her eyes. Just as our fingerprint is a one-of-a-kind representation of who we are, our personality is a distinct expression of our individuality.

We are created with a need for interaction and connection with others. Some people need more; some people need less. Those with the gift of gab are balanced in community with those who are by nature more introverted and introspective. With the proper awareness and operating environment, the strengths of one person balances out the weaknesses of another. With concentrated effort on our part, we can put the masks aside and initiate an open environment for true communication and healthy connections.

While reading a devotional, the following words jumped off the page, "We protect ourselves in dozens of ways from being exposed or known and thus remain closed people."[96] What a tragedy. Being known is a large part of the human experience. Being accepted and understood brings a sense of completeness and fulfillment into our lives. Everyone chooses whether to step toward empowering connections or remain in isolation. We have total control over who we allow into our inner circle of intimacy and who we choose to keep behind our protective fence.

It saddens me when I see people closing themselves off from God and from people under the weight of an overwhelming internal burden. They are stuck in a constant struggle and won't let anyone in to help!

I have experienced the isolation deception myself. Living with alcoholism as an early childhood backdrop hindered my ability to give and receive love. This was later compounded by mental abuse by another authority figure; I withdrew further into isolation. My ability to trust and connect was unfortunately replaced by an abnormal fear of healthy bonding with others. Even though I felt trapped and alone because I was afraid to rely on anyone, I needed the help of God and other people to extract myself from a self-induced, sneaky snare of seclusion. What a catch-22! I needed people to help me learn to trust people again.

Freedom and intimate connection with God enables me to encourage those around me.[97] I now willingly give and receive love. What a turnaround!

Remaining in a closed emotional state comes at a high price. Who would want to live a life closed off from true connection to God, when He is the source not only of all life, but the source of the answers we need? If we let down our defenses and consider the timeless truth God is good, He will prove himself. One of the bravest prayers can be, "If you are real, God, show me." Another helpful prayer is, "I give up; please help me, Father!" After we get out of the way, it is amazing what He is able to accomplish. God loves to hear us ask, "Abba, who do You say that I am?" His vision for our lives is always positive, affirming, and empowering.

In the jungle of life, it is easy to become wary of people because of their hurtful knack of bumping into our weaknesses with one of their imperfections. On the other side of this coin, these people bring new ideas, creativity, logic, and love into our sphere which adds color to our world. The joy of knowing others and being known ourselves far outweighs the pain of learning to accept and deal with personality flaws and human slip-ups.

Choose relationship; loving, strong friendships are nourishing, satisfying, and rewarding.

Opening Destiny's Door

We each hold our personal destiny in our hands. Our lives are the product of our thinking. We have the life we believe for. We cannot let fear, doubt or shame spoken by others steal our courage from us. We should avoid hiding in dark corners, believing the lie we will be safer in seclusion. Although coping mechanisms may temporarily shelter us from attack, in excess they deceive us into watching our opportunities and future rewards pass us by.

Laughter, retreat, education, patience, and hard work are five healthy responses we can use to cope with difficult situations and relationships. Coping mechanisms can be used in a positive manner if we don't put our faith in them to ultimately protect or provide for us. The best way to cope with distress is to put our trust in God and learn to rest in Him until He tells us how to go forward. As we step forward into God-given assignments to use our God-given gifts expressed through our unique personality, we will fulfill our destinies.

Every major league baseball hitter knows they will strike out over fifty percent of the time. They keep on swinging because they also understand they will never hit the ball if they don't swing. Just like Babe Ruth, we keep swinging at the good pitches no matter what.

Until we unlock the doors and come out into the vast unknown, we will never find life's supreme treasures. It is how we live and what we invest our time in that matters.

Stay in relationship with others even when things don't always go right. Choose to identify and control any hindering coping mechanisms, open the door of opportunity in front of you, and see what lies ahead in that wonderful world of yours!

COMMUNICATE AND CONNECT

Roaarrr! In the Tanzanian animal reserve, the male lion roars to terrorize and tempt the gazelles into running. In the herd, they are safe; there is protection for the weak, old, and sick. Their instinct tells them to stay by their fellow gazelles. As the lion unleashes his thunderous cry, panic begins to reverberate inside his prey's mind and heart. The power of fear overcomes herd instinct.

As one bolts for cover, the lionesses move in for the kill. Isolation comes right before destruction. The wisdom of remaining in the herd becomes blatantly obvious. This is a fitting word picture about why we need friends and connections.

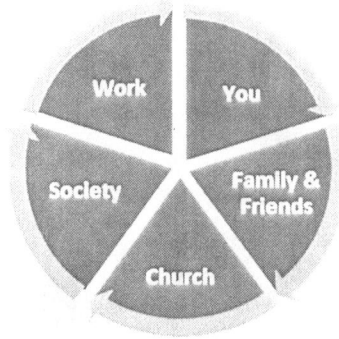

≋

We need other people. Family, friends, and social or work-related contacts are an essential part of a healthy life.

As we go through life, every person has a need for unconditional love and acceptance. In the deepest parts of our inner man, we desire to love and be loved. Even introverts want to be loved.

Being loved and accepted is a basic human need that begins with birth, extends through childhood, and lasts through adulthood. Babies who are not given attention during the first year of life develop severe attachment disorders or in some cases die. Young children sing a song or ride their bike, wobbles and all, down the sidewalk to hear the praise of their parents. Adolescents page through a family scrapbook yet again to be reminded of loving, positive memories of days gone by. In our hearts we all desire the love, blessing, and approval of our parents or mentors. We were created to receive this blessing to help propel us into adulthood.

The number one need for humans is love and acceptance.

We all long for positive experiences like knowing the pure, unconditional love of our first puppy, achieving a hard-fought victory, or hearing purpose-affirming encouragement from a significant person in our life. On the other extreme, many live through long, harsh, negative experiences of alcoholism, divorce, sickness or death of a loved one. Round that out with a dose of daily belittlement, mental abuse, or disappointments, and a person can feel misused. Both positive and negative experiences play a pivotal role in how we view the world and how we feel about ourselves.

When I was in college, I traveled as a student representative to a nationwide convention in New Orleans for computer professionals. I was in the throes of deciding whether I wanted to continue on my career path toward NASA or make a serious commitment in my current dating relationship. Due to the divergent locations for each path, I couldn't do both.

While at the convention, young computer professionals congregated around me wherever I started a conversation. These smart and talented professionals, so busy with their demanding careers, craved human contact. In spite of their financial success, most of them were lonely and starved for companionship. I decided love would be a more satisfying reward than the money and stuff I could own.

Choose a life rich in love, family, and friends.

Communicating and Listening

The laws of communication and connection are powerful. In order to cultivate the skills necessary to relate feelings and concepts to other people, remember the law of connection: To connect with others, find common ground. We build a shared reality by understanding and acknowledging the point of view of others. Solid connections are formed through listening and affirming someone's value as a person.

Good communication always has lanes going in both directions. After considering the timing for our conversation and what we want to say, we should prepare our hearts to listen to our friend's message. With honesty shown out of care and concern, we gently nudge each other to consider all the options and address sticky situations. As faithful friends, we prod one another along in taking the necessary action to solve problems we might otherwise ignore. Acquaintances become close comrades by working together to succeed in the messy battles of life.

The law of connection is sabotaged when we make assumptions, act arrogant or indifferent, or demand to be in control all the time. It is a mistake to assume we know what another person is thinking or feeling. When we presume other people think like us and have lived through experiences similar to ours, it is easy to project what we feel and think onto what they are saying. These type of assumptions easily pave the way for a blowup or misunderstanding, which causes friction, strife, discord, and division. If we see one of these trouble spots approaching, we need a tool to disarm and address the conflict.

Active Listening

The skill of active listening is a simple and effective tool to ensure good communication. Active listening is consciously and deliberately listening to another person with the goal of hearing and comprehending the intended *meaning* of the words spoken. We can develop the required skill set by practicing the entire active listening process. Using this tool will close the communication gap in our personal and business lives. When we are not getting our message across or sense frustration in someone else, we can take out the tool of active listening and easily get back on track.

A Process that Works

The active listening process is based on consciously tuning your ears to listen to what the other person is conveying and summarizing the message back to them. Here is a simple example of how active listening might help solve an argument in real life:

He's late and didn't call again! Aggravated, Sally looked out the window while she washed dishes. *He just doesn't care,* she thought.

Later, with the children sleeping, tempers flared at the kitchen table. "How many times have I asked you to call if you're going to be late?"

"I'm sorry," apologized her husband, slumping in the chair.

"Sorry? Is sorry supposed to fix it? The supper I slaved over turned to mush. If you cared, you'd at least try to call. I have asked a hundred times, but you never do!"

"You're at it again. You always think the worst of me. Look, when I saw the schedule I thought about calling, but then I got busy with the last bunch of customers. It took way longer than I thought. As soon as I finished, I grabbed my bag and rushed home. I didn't think about calling again until I was out of the parking lot." Throwing up his hands in exasperation, he went to put his bag in the living room.

Following him, Sally replied sarcastically, "Really." Her eyes rolled as she crossed her arms. "You could have dialed at the stoplight."

With a deep sigh, he turned to face her. "My phone battery was dead. I just wanted to get home. I did the best I could. I knew this wouldn't end well."

The light bulb suddenly came on inside Sally's head; she realized she wasn't listening. Calming herself, she offered, "So, am I hearing you say that even though you didn't call, you wanted to get home on time?"

"Yes, that is what I am trying to say. I have to stay until the last customer leaves."

"Honey, are you saying you're late even though you don't want to be when customers come in near closing?"

Feeling heard, he walked toward Sally. "Yes, that's what I am saying. Of course I want to come home as soon as I can; you and the kids are the reason I work so hard."

Sally sank into his arms, "I'm sorry for being crabby. By suppertime, I really need a break and can't wait to see your face walk through the door. To me, it is worth the two extra minutes to stop and call. I need you to call if at all possible. Would you forgive me for yelling at you?"

"Yes, I forgive you. I'm sorry, too. If it means that much to you, I'll try to call next time."

We have the power to change the tone of any argument the moment we choose to listen. The power of active listening can change the atmosphere and help to lower the defenses of both people. When we really hear each other's point of view, a solution is usually right around the corner.

When we experience a breakdown in communication, some people find it helpful to slow the process down by clearly defining the speaking and listening roles. If we are constantly interrupting or not able to focus on what the other person is saying, we can assign someone the speaker role by having them hold a simple object like a pen. There is only one speaker at a time; the other person's job is to listen to gain understanding. When we concentrate only on listening and repeating back what was communicated, the process increases the likelihood of mutual understanding.

The active listening process is simple. Whoever is currently speaking *has the floor* and holds a small object such as a pen. The listener focuses on hearing the speaker's perspective, especially if it isn't what he or she *wants* to hear. When the speaker is done talking, he or she transfers the right to speak by handing the pen to the listener. The listener paraphrases what they have heard the speaker say. The pen is given back to the speaker who will either confirm the listener has heard correctly or give the listener more details until the speaker's message becomes clear. As the two people alternate in exploring one side of the issue, the cycle with the pen continues until the concept has been transmitted and received correctly.

After the first person's point of view has successfully been heard, the listener and the speaker switch roles. The process repeats itself until the second person's point of view has also been fully communicated. A solution usually presents itself during the process of both people cooperating to be heard.

People naturally connect with others who are there to listen and help–rather than air their superiority. Make sure the conversation focuses on the other person and what they need in order to succeed. If we feel we know more than the other person, we come across as arrogant. We won't make any friends by being condescending or egotistical. It is often helpful to offer what we know or have experienced to encourage the other person, but don't go overboard or fall into the trap of bragging. After letting others decide what to do with the input, we have the privilege of celebrating with them when they bring us news of their victory.

Active listening communicates interest.

Listening can be hard work. If we keep one eye on our computer, TV or cell phone while we are talking with people, we silently scream a lack of interest in what they are sharing. For important conversations, eye contact with the other person communicates active interest. Don't rush through the silences; just enjoy being in their presence.

Waiting for the other person's response communicates honor to them.

When we take the time to pay attention, it conveys we care. Caring means much more than anything else we could do for them. Having someone else take the time to listen is sometimes all a friend needs at the moment.

Friendships are forged when we seek to understand other people and what they need. True friends take the time to ask us key questions even if they sense the process might cause conflict or confrontation. It is wise to consider beforehand what would be the right time and atmosphere for any one-on-one talk that might extend into sensitive issues. To prepare what we want to say in advance, we ask the Holy Spirit for wisdom in choosing what exact words to use and what not to say.

When making a friend or connecting with a new contact, we should respect their need to set their own boundaries and to accept or reject our input. No one likes to be in a conversation that feels like a master commanding a slave what to do. We can only offer to connect; they have to want to connect and engage willingly with us. By its very definition, friendship cannot be forced or gained through manipulation. They will reject us if they feel like the direction is headed down a one-way path.

How we perceive each other is crucial to crafting a win-win conversation. If someone expects and projects rejection into every conversation, the connection will remain fractured. Entering into a relationship with the need to cling to the other person out of insecurity will suffocate the relationship. No one can interact with others in a healthy manner all the time; however, behaviors driven by insecurity interfere with our success in making friends and connections.

The bottom line is this: when we communicate with others, we need to connect first and allow the conversation to progress with both people fully engaged and invested in the outcome. Make an effort not only to transmit facts, but to connect with the heart and message of the other person. The outcome is often surprising and refreshing.

When we join hearts with someone else, it creates an open door. As we create the opportunity by being vulnerable ourselves, it lowers the risk level for the other individual to let their guard down and invites them closer. We nurture true bonds with other people when we share from the heart. A family-like kinship results because of our natural preference for each other.

Reach out your hand to offer a human touch.

Sharing from the heart may not be easy because it involves risk. The benefits of sharing, however, far outweigh the costs. How do you start sharing? *Be brave enough to listen to what your heart is saying and be bold enough to let your voice be heard.* Offering what you think and feel will draw out a similar response from the other person; sweet communication naturally flows as ideas are exchanged. A shared reality begins to form.

Every day we see the powerful principle of exchange in society. Money is exchanged for ideas, physical assets, materials, ownership rights, food, transportation, communication tools, services, and many other things. One of the strengths of our country is the ability to exchange through commerce. Products are grown or produced and exchanged many times over. In nature and in commerce, we see a cycle of synergy and exchange. We are a cog in this wheel.

Our individual lives depend on the exchange between each other. When we have a support network of friends and connections, we are stronger. Have you ever tried to break a rope of three cords braided together? They are tough. I tried this once with three long, braided dandelion stems and couldn't break or rip it. We gain inner peace and confidence when our relationships are healthy enough to openly give and receive love even in times of stress.

Avoiding Out-of-Balance Responses

Balance is a stabilizing force because it keeps us out of unhealthy extremes.

Pain produces similar responses in people of all places, in all times, of all ages. Powerful physical, psychological, social, and mental defense mechanisms kick in as we live through painful experiences. Depending on the severity, we may come out with only a wound that heals over time or we may see a noticeable scar for the rest of our lives. If the pain is beyond our ability to cope, we may even develop personality or attachment disorders; our views of the world might become skewed, biased, and out of balance. No matter what, we are all responsible for our responses and the consequences that follow.

I write this with the voice of experience. I had problems with attachment to other people from an extreme lack of trust and fear of risk. In order to cope with the things I had seen and suffered through as a child, I had unknowingly created a strongbox and locked the trauma and fear tightly away as a way to defend and preserve myself. As the prison doors swung shut, I was trapped and couldn't seem to find the exit. I wanted to trust others, but I couldn't make myself. The lie of irrational self-preservation became my law of survival.

If you are trapped and want to escape and break free, it is my desire to help you. Here are some out-of-balance responses to avoid.

Isolation

Choosing a life of isolation is unhealthy because it limits our input streams during times of tragedy or unexpected attack. It is unhealthy to be an island unto ourselves. Without being around people to bounce ideas off of, we are forced into operating in a vacuum, without other human voices to offer advice. Before God created Eve, He said, "It is not good man should be alone."[98] The influence of family and friends brings equilibrium into our lives as we navigate the system of weights and balances. The result is stability and poise as we navigate through life's changes and challenges.

When the lion roars, "Nobody understands you. No one loves you. Nobody is there for you. Nobody cares," stay in the herd. If we try to operate in isolation, we have no options for support when we are in distress. When trapped in our self-obsession, we also miss opportunities to support someone else in their rebuilding. It is important to participate in the process of exchange. Healthy interchange allows for the multiplication of ideas and trading of resources.

Avoidance

Avoiding nourishing, interdependent relationships is unhealthy. Many dysfunctional people want to receive from someone or something without giving anything in exchange. This makes no sense because it is in the give and take we grow and gain understanding. Before my first makeover, I avoided exchanging with others because I didn't trust them or myself. My spirit of lack was so dominant I sometimes used others to get what I needed. Not only did I cheat myself from the blessing of giving, but also from developing mutual friendships through which I could later tap into for needed resources.

Mistrust

Mistrust is a toxin that contaminates how we see opportunities. It is self-defeating to assign selfish motives or ill-intent to others during every conversation or encounter we have. When we constantly focus on what could go wrong, we feel the need to protect ourselves from imaginary attacks. Fear and dread pollute our contact with others, become a self-fulfilling prophecy of rejection, and propagate a victim mentality.

When we withhold our gifts and abilities from others who need them, we deny them our assistance to flourish. Our mistrust not only holds them back but limits our possibilities for the future.

When we share with others who we are, including our skills and abilities, it allows for our gifts to make a way for us in the future. It might seem like keeping our talents to ourselves is the smart choice, but doing the exact opposite is what activates the power of God's kingdom in our life. Using our time and talents in positive and productive ways allows our God-given potential to bloom forth into a full-grown tree of life. With a vision of the plentiful harvest ahead, we can push mistrust out of the way and agree in our heart to hope, trust, and freely give.

Obsession

We can also tip out of balance by being overly dependent or sharing too much too fast in a relationship. Have you ever met someone who is lonely, but when you reach out a hand of friendship, she latches on to you and texts you every hour or incessantly messages you on Facebook? Like approaching a drowning swimmer, you become their life preserver. Their panic and obsessive behavior can threaten to pull you under. Part of a lifesaving course is learning how to save someone without letting them drown you during the rescue. Offer your assistance, but enforce a balanced approach which teaches independence and responsibility. Their ultimate source of value and help must come from God and depend upon a balanced set of relationships.

Codependence

Another trap of unhealthy relationships is thinking if we can convince someone to love us, we will feel fulfilled. This is a huge blinking-red warning sign. If we carry around a gaping God-sized hole and expect a person to meet our need instead of God, we are in for a massive disappointment. Our internal fuel tank cannot be met by pilfering off someone else's life. One of the fastest ways to kill a relationship that has potential is to suck off someone else's energy like a parasite. No one else can make us happy; we choose to be happy. After we take responsibility for our happiness, then we are free to share our life and support each other.

Just like in team building, friendships need to undergo a natural progression. Healthy relationships have a give and take with many unspoken, unwritten boundaries. In emergencies we tend to arrange our lives around meeting a certain need. When the crisis is over, however, our priorities need to come back into order as we balance faith, family, work, and outside commitments.

Agreement in Relationship

Being in the right relationships is a key component in making progress toward our goals and recovering from setbacks. Meriwether Louis and his childhood friend, William Clark, explored together as they crossed mountains, rivers, and the unknown western expansion to chart a route to the Pacific Ocean. Where would Batman be without the support of his faithful sidekick, Robin? We are stronger when we operate in close connection with someone who will support and defend us. Allowing confidants deeper access into our lives creates rapport. This bonding makes both parties more powerful and resilient.

Two acting in agreement will always produce more than each can produce separately. The other person may be able to contribute a better idea than you could think of on your own. Their sharp idea plus one of your clever ideas may be exactly what you both need to accelerate down the road to success. The power comes through complementing each other's strengths and weaknesses and staying in unity.

Assuming Good Motives

There are many benefits to identifying the true motivation behind what people say and do. If we incorrectly assume someone is acting from a harmful motive, we imagine they said things they never said or implied. Things go better if we presume good motives. This illustrates one of the most powerful truths about communication: How you perceive a thing is how you will receive a thing.

Perception determines reception.

To explore the power of determining good motive, let's take a closer look at a mother's innocent suggestion, "Let's go shopping; you need some new clothes."

If we assign a favorable motive to the mother, we might respond, "Fantastic idea, I like shopping. Even though this is my favorite shirt, if I'm honest, I admit it's looking kinda rough." Another version might sound like, "Wow, I'm glad you offered. I can always use another eye-catching shirt!" The positive vibes are coming through. If we don't want to go shopping, we can still be cooperative and communicate what we are feeling in a positive way. "Thanks so much for the offer. I certainly appreciate it, but I have all the clothes I need right now."

If we assume bad motive to the mother, our thoughts might go in this direction, *She doesn't like my clothes. I'm never good enough for her,* or *I'm tired of her constant criticism. I'm fine—I like looking like this.* Can you hear the negative assumptions about what the mother meant by her suggestion?

Blaming others for both real and imagined hurts can become our normal mode of operation. Our negative thoughts can be compared to a common lawn weed, the dandelion. Merely pinching off the leaves, stem, and yellow top doesn't kill the pesky weed. Dandelions have a long primary root feeding the beasts from below. Like the unwanted dandelion, we systematically remove negative thoughts, which have deep-seated roots in lies, through exposure to the truth of the Bible. The Holy Spirit guides us to the truth and the truth sets us free.[99]

Like colors in the rainbow that perfectly complement one another, our friends and connections add beauty and texture to the backdrop of our lives. By learning to connect and communicate, we can create a balanced, enjoyable life and reach agreement in essential areas with the core people in our lives. We can dislodge the strife and confusion, which threatens to tear apart our relationships, by utilizing active listening and team-building concepts to resolve conflicts. Just as the colors of the rainbow merge seamlessly into one another, our interactions with family, friends, mentors, and associates paint a canvas of living color.

LEAVE A LEGACY

There was a survey which asked people eighty years and older what they would have done differently with their lives if they had the chance. Out of the hundreds of answers offered, three answers were the most dominant:

1. Reflect more.
2. Risk more.
3. Do things that will last beyond your lifetime.

Reflect More

Reflection is a powerful tool when used in the right way for the right reasons.

The practice of personal reflection is a lost art. When we travel at breakneck speed, we sometimes repeat the same heartbreaking mistakes. The overcommitted have no time to find solutions to their problems; they keep patching the holes. When we choose to step back and wait before taking action, our vision clears and the fog begins to lift. The non-committed wait around wishing things were different. In an effort to hide from reality, some find it easier to lose themselves in a fantasy world or imagine things are different than they really are.

After extracting ourselves from the snare of wishful thinking through reflection, we can take bold steps to effect change. With a higher vision, our thoughts rise to a level that is both informed and achievable.

Achieving Clarity of Focus

As we take the time to consider and mull over recent happenings, clarity settles in. Through the keen eyes of analysis, we see the reality of what has been happening. Necessary actions come into focus.

As godly wisdom cultivates the fruit of self-appraisal and self-control, we can stop the destruction brought on by out of control emotions. The -*dom* in wisdom comes from the root word meaning dominion. When we put that with the root word *wise*, we take dominion by applying wisdom. With wisdom as our established base, we can make smarter decisions with confidence.

Our knee-jerk, emotional roller-coaster style of living ends when we take the time to consider circumstances from all relevant points of view. Many times our true motivations are revealed. Reflection causes us to pause long enough to admit when we have made a mistake and need to apologize, change direction, or start anew. Reflection creates an opening for wisdom and discipline to enter in.

Shaping a Healthier Response

An honest evaluation of our conversations or disagreements with others can lead to changes in how we express ourselves. After reviewing the outcome of a recent argument, we may realize we inadvertently used a harsh voice tone as we let our emotions rage out of control. An apology may be in order. Sometimes our tone of voice can be very negative if we feel disrespected or offended during a misunderstanding. Another benefit of personal reflection can be realizing when we communicated a message we did not intend or would not appreciate receiving ourselves. In each of these cases, the tool of reflection leads us to an opportunity to offer an apology and repair the damage. After evaluating our past reactions, we can use our conclusions to shape a healthier response in the future.

Learning From Our Past

History repeats itself unless we learn from our past. After suffering a heartbreak or betrayal, many people create a plan for revenge. Retaliation is a trap because it perpetuates the cycle. Others fall into the sink hole of regret from the weight of past mistakes. Regret sucks them in like quicksand. By sidestepping traps like revenge and refusing to wallow in regret, we are in a position to learn and put our energy into our makeover. As we spend more time reflecting, a clearer, more accurate image appears.

Mistakes are the portals of discovery. (Unknown)

Learning from others' mistakes. In our daily living, people we know, work with, or dearly love make mistakes that are painful to watch and difficult to recover from. By careful observation, we can gather knowledge from their blunders; we can avoid making similar mistakes. Without reflection, we cannot learn from the pain borne from someone else's wrong thinking. By studying their lives, we can gain wisdom from their missteps and their successes.

Benjamin Franklin said, "An ounce of prevention is worth a pound of cure." I say an ounce of reflection is worth a pound of recovery.

Risk More

Fighter pilots, skydivers, and Indy race car drivers all have one thing in common: they love taking risks. To them, the thrill of victory is worth the agony of defeat and all of the danger. They are bored with the mundane. These professionals live on the far side of the risk scale. When should taking chances come into play in the life of the average person?

When we are young, many of us are infatuated with dreams, full of risk and adventure, which propel us toward an unknown, idealistic future. In one fell swoop, life can throw us a curveball and deflate our naïve balloons. The pain of an unexpected defeat jolts us awake and pushes us over on the scale from acceptable risk to extreme caution. This is normal and even beneficial as long as we don't become trapped there.

Without risk, our dreams will never become a reality. If we insulate ourselves from all possible harm, we stay trapped and slowly suffocate. Without the desire to take steps out of our comfort zone, many times our potential remains untapped and undeveloped. Especially during the perilous periods of our lives, we have to embrace change and the possibility of failure. In order to climb up, over, and into a new territory, we have to face the unknown. To take steps of faith, we need a willing heart.

I can't think of a situation where there is more risk and more need of hope than at the Olympics. Hopeful Olympians carry within themselves a gigantic dream. Future Olympians foresee hundreds and hundreds of days of practice and sacrifice between them and the gold medal. Each day contains moments when they stand on the brink of disaster. A new skill or level of difficulty is not mastered without leaps of faith. Why do we dream with the athletes every four years as they put their life's work on display? We wish we could be like them, risking it all for the gold medal. Take a chance to grow and expand—Go for it!

We all face moments of decision as we wind our way through life. Will we press courageously forward, in spite of everything, or will we stay where we are? In a scene near the end of the movie *Pay It Forward,* a twelve-year-old boy, Dylan, describes what we might wrestle with during such a moment, "Some people are too scared. I guess it's hard for some people who are used to things the way they are to change. They kinda give up. When they do, everybody loses."[100]

Keep declaring, "With God's help, I can!"

Taking Chances

Many people drive by places they would love to visit but don't venture off the beaten path to follow their heart's desire. Every day people walk by special people they could be famous friends with, but they don't consider stopping by to say hello. When you see an opportunity before you, I urge you to *cross over the chicken line*[101] with your courage firmly in hand. Take a risk and see what happens.

Arriving at a small town rodeo as a child, I watched in amazement as the bull thrashed; its only goal was to rid itself of its rider. To take life by the horns and develop decision muscles, we take on the obvious risks to pursue the exciting rewards of our own bull ride. To face our rodeo challenges, we need boldness to uncover the courage deep down inside to really live. To gain our reward, we quit hiding outside the arena and compete with the goal of finishing our ride well.

Facing the luck of the draw, the bull rider skillfully applies all the expertise he possesses. The rider cannot inspect the bull he drew and say, "I don't like this bull, I want a redraw." He has to make the best of his draw, plan his strategy, and use every trick and well-practiced skill to attempt an eight-second ride. As we face the luck of the draw in life, we move forward in bold faith that God has equipped us with everything we need.

Like the bull rider, we cannot control every influence that will affect the outcome of our efforts. We need to be willing to push forward in order to succeed. Our fear of failure and the unknown can be overcome by taking action even when we are afraid. We cannot allow anxiety to paralyze us or prevent us from putting forth the effort needed to give ourselves the chance to enjoy our lives.

Facing Failure and Setbacks

Setbacks are a part of every person's life. We don't enjoy the battle, but we endure and push past obstacles. Learning from our failures gives us an increased chance at success.

As Thomas Edison was struggling to invent the light bulb, he saw the essential value in his failed attempts. Mr. Edison's statement perfectly describes what I am trying to say: "I have not failed. I've just found 10,000 ways that won't work."[102] Thomas Edison knew every unsuccessful experiment brought him one step closer to seeing his invention come to life as he ruled out one unworkable idea after another. He refused to label his efforts as failures. Because of his daily determination to overcome all obstacles in his way, we have enjoyed the light bulb for over one hundred years.

When we face failure or a roadblock, we need to have the courage to say, "I will try again tomorrow." Not every day will be glamorous or flashy, but that sort of bravery keeps us making progress and speaks volumes to those around us.

The Value of Hope

What keeps some people from taking a risk and going for it? A lack of hope. Many feel so defeated they do not have the capacity for optimism. The wellspring of courage has run dry because the level of expectation and faith to try has run out. Hope is essential for the human race to advance. One of the saddest sentences I ever heard uttered by a person living in defeat is, "Hope is dangerous." What a mouthful in three words. Can anything express despair and a lack of anticipation any clearer?

When we lack hope, it is evident we need another touch of God's love. His touch can restore our confidence that something beautiful, though challenging, is possible. Anticipation can be a fragile thing when we are in recovery or distress. God's encouragement can touch our heart to dream again. The strength of friends and family can sustain us long enough to find our positivity again. Our Father's love gives us the strength to expect something more. No matter how corrupt things appear, we can refuse to envision life through the veil of fear, dread, or lack.

If we open our heart and mind to what is possible, we can use the power of focused, faith-filled words and actions to establish what we have been believing for. Even in the midst of trials and extreme stress, blessings are on the way if you are a believer.

When a teenager is snowboarding or skateboarding, what do they do when they crash? They suffer through some stitches and are back at it as soon as the headache is over. How do we recover when we take a risk, fall, and injure our pride? Just like a persistent teenager, we bandage our wounds and keep going. We choose to go for it in spite of our loss and the fear of the unknown. I would like to offer an aggressive life motto that can push us to take necessary risks when we are at a crossroads.

Overcome fear by taking the first step.

Take the First Step

We can overcome our fear of the unknown, failure, rejection, and disapproval by continuing to pray, prepare, and courageously take the first step toward our goal. At the beginning of a new venture, we don't know how it will turn out. We can't always predict what someone else's reaction will be to our new idea or direction. It is easier to stay in the game if we envision a desirable outcome.

With a goal in mind, make the best plans possible and gather all of the available resources.

It is easy to appraise someone else's success and think they were confident of every step they took along the way. This couldn't be further from the truth. As we move along the path, we listen for God's voice, look for signs, and make the best faith-filled decisions possible.

With our voice of courage, we can stop skepticism from smothering our dreams. Any self-doubt which prevents our advancement can be dismantled by stepping out with actions that combine risk tempered with wisdom and self-control. Doubt and fear are normal human emotions that need to be acknowledged and managed. If they are allowed to steer the train engine of our lives, we will be in for one wicked ride. Successful people keep doubt and fear in the caboose and let their faith, voice, talents, and abilities take them to their desired destination.

Where do you want your next destination to be?

Under Pressure, Build Relationship

Stress and risk can be powerful influences for all types of change. A speaker at a seminar I attended shared that camping is an invaluable family-building activity. Visions of soaking wet sleeping bags and of repeatedly walking to pump water into five-gallon containers flashed through my mind. Were these great family-building activities? Was he crazy? His explanation surprised me. He claimed that as families conquered stressful situations together, the struggle helps the family unit to bond and pull together.

As I considered his answer, past memories of our family's many camping and hiking experiences flashed by. I remembered when our family had gotten drenched hiking to the top of Vernal Falls. During another stormy camping weekend, we had huddled together and embellished the past as lightning flashed all around our tent.

One after another, a familiar slide show of memories flashed by; I nodded in silent agreement. Making s'mores and tinfoil dinners over the fire along with midnight trips to the bathroom by flashlight had bonded us together and helped to build a shared sense of identity.

Continuing to strengthen relationships can help us cope when we face risky situations that cause us to struggle. Whether it is rafting the rapids of the Grand Canyon in flash flood conditions, suffering through unexpected unemployment caused by layoffs, or undergoing a surgery due to a life-threatening illness, facing risk and the accompanying stress can pull relationships closer together or push them apart. In our families, churches, communities, and work groups, we can either adapt to stress in a positive way or let the stress create havoc.

When I notice myself starting to overreact under stress, one useful coping mechanism I use is to come to a complete stop; I refuse to say or do anything I will later regret. This gives me time to resist the desire to isolate myself or lash out at someone. Waiting for my emotions to calm down also limits the amount of damage I unleash on others or create for myself. Once I relax and come back to my senses, I look for positive routes I can take instead. My goal is to find a way to work with other people toward a solution.

To initiate an effective makeover, transformation is needed which means change is inevitable. Many maturing experiences are wrapped in a threat which requires us to move under pressure. How we respond to the perceived threat determines how we are affected. If we accept that uncertainty almost always accompanies this type of growth, we are more likely to break through the anxiety barrier and cross over. Danger can either stimulate us to build new relationships and expand into new territory or to malfunction and demolish what we already have.

Courage is not the absence of fear, but choosing a faith response in the midst of challenging circumstances. Don't hide, run or malfunction when pressure comes, but use the power of bold bravery to jump in to your incredible life makeover.

Do Things That Last Beyond Your Lifetime

We hold our breath and bite our fingernail as the news plays video of a 747 scraping to a halt on the tarmac with no landing gear. We breathe a collective sigh of relief when we hear the passengers are safe. Why? Planes can be easily replaced with money; human lives cannot. Our material possessions may last beyond our lifetime, but in and of themselves they hold only a temporal value. In the beginning, God created man by breathing into his nostrils the breath of life.[103] All human life is sacred because we are made in the image of God and carry His nature.[104]

A well-lived life is characterized by healthy relationships and acts of love and service. My grandfather passed away at the age of ninety-three. Over two hundred and fifty family clan members honored his memory, accomplishments, and character at a small church in Cameron, Wisconsin. What did we consider noteworthy at our beloved's funeral? Through tears of sorrow, cherished memories were shared highlighting his generous heart and embracing love. My grandfather left a rich inheritance indeed.

Time is our life being poured out like an hourglass.

Use Time and Resources Wisely

Our schedules and assets are two paramount resources we are given to steward. What we spend our time and income on is an indication of what is important to us.

Time is one of our most valuable and finite resources. As one day passes, we cannot retrieve it. We can take what we learn and apply it to our next challenge, but we cannot change what is already past. We are not allowed redos, repeats, rewinds or do-overs in place of yesterday. The ticking of the clock measures the expenditure of our lives. What we spend our time on reveals where our priorities are.

This picture was taken at a women's meeting in one of the poorest compounds in Lusaka, Zambia. Declining the opportunity to become overseers over a group of churches, the pastor and his wife have chosen to stay with their small congregation, in spite of the level of poverty and suffering. Their love and humility touched my heart. Their acts of service demonstrate their priorities.

Time is money. Money is a slippery commodity to wrap our mind around. It can be used for extreme evil or tremendous gain. Many people spend their time, energy, and resources to make money, but later waste it on foolish temporal things. If someone reviews our checkbook, what we value will become obvious. When considering the purchase of an item, we mentally compare the price of what we are buying against how much time is needed to earn the money.

Have you ever considered that what you spend your money on is what your life was expended for? Keep your spending in check and use your income for something meaningful—every purchase is paid for with minutes, hours, or days of your life.

Sacrifice to Leave a Legacy

We should use our money and material possessions for more than our self-preservation and selfish gain. As led by the Holy Spirit, we should help our fellow man and support worthy projects and causes that will last beyond our lifetime.

We have national treasures such as Yosemite and the Grand Canyon because former presidents valued them enough to preserve them for our posterity. It is easy to reflect on such nature reserves and say, "Thank you, Mr. President, for securing such a national treasure for future generations to enjoy, including me and my family." We have no idea the pressure or stress they endured to leave a lasting legacy.

I think of the signers of the Declaration of Independence, men such as Thomas Jefferson and John Hancock, and how they signed their lives away for future generations. They knew if they were caught, they would be prosecuted and hanged for treason against England. The legacy of a free nation demanded risk and personal sacrifice.

As we voyage through life, we face character-building challenges that force us to make choices. Although most of us aren't out saving the world, our daily duties often push us to choose between taking the easy way out and making a sacrifice for the future. By choosing right over wrong, our influence can be felt as we invest our lives in meaningful tasks to leave an inheritance for posterity.

Practicing the art of reflection, risk-taking, and legacy-building is life changing. While we consider our ways, reflection steers us toward wisdom. As we trust in the Lord and courageously fight our battles, we grow into faith-filled risk-takers. Over a lifetime of loving God, ourselves, and others, we can craft a lasting legacy.

Reflect more; risk more; and do things that last beyond your lifetime. A daring adventure awaits you during your incredible life makeover.

DARE TO DREAM

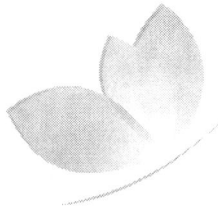

Without vision, the people will perish.
Without courage and inspiration, dreams will die.
Rosa Parks [105]

After studying daring historical figures like Rosa Parks, who overcame societal resistance to play a significant role in confronting racial prejudice in American culture, we see the importance of having a higher vision. Vision, when properly articulated, inspires courage; vision awakens the necessary passion to change our world. Our makeover will be directly affected by our ability to see from a higher elevation. We cannot allow any negative filters or lenses to block our field of vision. Perception is a key to seeing our dreams become a reality.

When we raise our focus above difficult circumstances, we can see what is possible. Vision is being able to articulate the picture we see in our mind. This is easy to do when we are at peace; it is hard to do when we are surrounded by danger. God's vision for humanity is based on freedom, abundance, and health. But in a fallen world, this certainly isn't the case for everyone.

As His children however, our actions should be directed toward walking out a mission, which aligns with God's vision, even amidst chaos.

Many Bible characters have risen from the ashes of defeat. In Jesus' greatest time of need, Peter denied even knowing Jesus.[106] Peter rose from the ashes of cowardice to later preach and saw three thousand people accept Christ in one day. The Christian-murdering Pharisee, Saul, was transformed into the apostle Paul through a God encounter. He wrote thirteen books of the New Testament and spread the message of Christ to Jews and Gentiles. After killing an Egyptian and being exiled, Moses rose from the ashes of obscurity as a shepherd in Midian to lead the nation of Israel to the Promised Land.[107]

Our past defeats that led to sorrow and ashes will not have the power to determine our destiny if we think and act differently. We need vision to dream for a new tomorrow.

Why do movies like *Iron Will*,[108] *We Are Marshall*,[109] *Lord of the Rings*,[110] and *Star Trek*[111] continue to thrill audiences year after year? In the epic struggles played out on the screen, the heroes portray the optimism, endurance, and commitment we hope to walk out in our lives. We need a higher vision, based on God's highest and best, to inspire us to fight for our life-changing makeover.

In spite of overwhelming odds, we too must doggedly run through the night and fight through the pain like Will Stoneman in *Iron Will*.[112] When we face punishing losses, we can emerge from the ashes of grief to grab glory if we act with the same courage as the Marshall[113] football team. Inspired by Frodo's quest in *Lord of the Rings*[114], we press on to shoulder our allotted burden and face our nemesis with resolve, regardless of the cost. We adopt the vision of the *Star Trek*[115] crew to "Boldly go where no man or woman has gone before!" Now is the time to dream.

Daring to Dream

One of the end goals of our transformation is to be able to dream with Father God: dream about what we want to become, what we want to accomplish, and how we can positively impact the world around us. Our incredible life makeover becomes possible by:

- The depth of relationship we build with Father, Son, and Holy Spirit;
- The kingdom values we choose to embody; and
- The choices we make every day.

Today is the day to find more meaning and purpose for our lives. It is time to dream again. If it seems impossible, choose to dream and refuse to let go. If it seems too hard, choose to dream and keep pressing forward. If you feel like quitting, go for your dream and never give up.

Makeover Miracles

If you have lost a child, I weep with you.
If you have survived the death of your parent(s) or spouse, I grieve with you.
If you have suffered through a divorce, I mourn with you.
If you have said goodbye to the house of your dreams, I cry with you.
If you have been devastated by unemployment, I wait with you.
If you have declared bankruptcy, I hurt with you.
If you have lost your health, I suffer with you.
If you have lost all hope, I ache with you.
But when the tears have all fallen, and we have wiped our cheeks, we go to God.

God wants to be the author and finisher of your incredible life makeover.

God wants to guide you by the Holy Spirit,

To step out of the shackles,
To put your past behind you,
To form a new identity within you,
To receive a new heart and a new mind,
To equip you to win the power struggles, and
To co-labor with you in kingdom living
so you may take your place in the Earth as a
much loved son or daughter of the Most High.

God wants to laugh with you, cry with you, speak with you, and dream with you. He wants to see you happy. He wants to see you whole. He wants to partner with you in your incredible life makeover. With God, all things are possible!

APPENDIX A

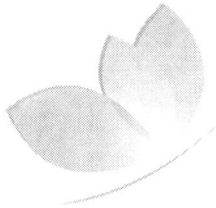

I am God's special treasure. Malachi 3:17.
No weapon formed against me shall prosper. Isaiah 54:17.
The Holy Spirit leads and guides me today. Romans 8:14.
I am more than a conqueror; I am an overcomer. Romans 8:37.
I have abundant life in Christ. John 10:10.
I am a doer of the Word and not a hearer only. James 1:22.
I have the mind of Christ. 1 Corinthians 2:16.
I take every thought captive and make it obey Christ. 2 Corinthians 10:5.
My mind is transformed by the renewing of my mind by the Word of God. Romans 12:2.
I will meditate on the Word of God day and night. Psalms 1:2.
I can do all things through Christ who strengthens me. Philippians 4:13.
I speak the truth of the Word of God in love. Ephesians 4:18.
I think on things that are good, pure, perfect, lovely, and of good report. Philippians 4:8.
I delight myself in the Lord. Psalms 37:4.

God supplies all my needs according to His riches in glory. Philippians 4:19.

I confess I am healed and whole. Psalms 103:3.

I am made in an amazing and wonderful way. Psalms 139:14.

I will always have everything I need because the Lord is my shepherd. Psalms 23:1.

I am never alone because God will never leave or forsake me. Deuteronomy 31:6.

I love the Lord, my God, with all my heart, soul, mind, and strength. Mark 12:30.

ENDNOTES

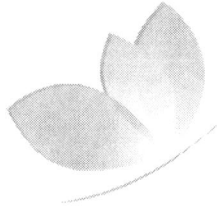

1. Isaiah 55:9 (*The Message*).
2. 1 John 4:18 (*New King James Version*).
3. 1 Corinthians 13:7-8 (*J.B. Phillips New Testament*).
4. Matthew 6:12 (NKJV).
5. Dann Stadler, *Angels in the Fire* (Bloomington: Bethany House Publishers, 2013), 68.
6. Mark 11:25 (*New International Version*).
7. Proverbs 18:21 (NKJV).
8. Liberty Savard, *Breaking the Power* (Gainesville: Bridge-Logos Publishers, 1997), 120-121.
9. Kris and Jason Vallotton, *The Supernatural Power of Forgiveness* (Ventura: Regal Books, 2011), 1-205.
10. R.T. Kendall, *Total Forgiveness*, rev.ed. (Lake Mary: Charisma House; Revised edition, 2007), 1-224.
11. Hebrews 12:29 (*Amplified Bible*).
12. Revelation 22:17, Ephesians 5:24-32 (NKJV).
13. Jeremiah 1:5 (AMP).
14. Psalms 139:13 (NKJV).
15. Psalms 139:14 (*New American Standard Bible*).

16. Hebrews 13:20-21 (AMP).
17. Colossians 2:11-15 (AMP).
18. 1 Corinthians 13:7-8 (AMP).
19. John 10:10 (AMP).
20. Psalms 51:10, 12 (AMP).
21. Psalms 51:6-7 (AMP).
22. Dr. Larry D. Stephens, *Please Let Me Know You, God*, (Nashville: Thomas Nelson Publishers, 1993) 250.
23. Psalms 91:14 (NKJV).
24. Dave Roever, *Scars That Heal: The True Life Story of Dave Roever* (World Wide Pictures Home Video, 1993), VHS.
25. Psalms 143:6, 8,10; Isaiah 29:13, 15 (AMP).
26. Mark 10:18 (AMP).
27. Luke 9:18, 28; Matthew 26:36 (AMP).
28. Luke 4:1 (AMP).
29. Luke 3:22, 4:4, 8, 12-13 (AMP).
30. Luke 4:14 (AMP).
31. John 10:10 (AMP).
32. Psalms 91:1-13 (MSG).
33. 1 Corinthians 13:4-5 (AMP).
34. 1 Corinthians 13:7 (NKJV).
35. 1 Corinthians 13:8 (*Good News Translation*).
36. Philippians 4:13 (NKJV).
37. Matthew 22:39 (NKJV).
38. 2 Corinthians 5:17 (*New Living Translation*).
39. Hebrews 12:2 (NKJV).
40. Philippians 4:8 (*Expanded Bible*).
41. 2 Corinthians 10:5 (NKJV).
42. Caroline Leaf, *Who Switched Off My Brain: Controlling Toxic Thoughts and Emotions*, (Place of publication not identified: Improv Ltd., 2009), distributed by Thomas Nelson, 176.
43. Caroline Leaf, *Switch On Your Brain: The Key to Peak Happiness, Thinking and Health* (Grand Rapids: Baker Books, 2013), 240.

44. Joshua 1:8 (AMP).
45. Romans 8:1 (NKJV).
46. Joel 2:26-27; Romans 10:11 (NKJV).
47. Haggai 2:5 (NKJV).
48. James 4:7 (NKJV); James 4:7-10 (MSG).
49. Isaiah 55:11 (AMP).
50. John 16:13 (*New Life Version*).
51. Dawna De Silva, *Shifting Atmospheres*, www.ibethel.org.
52. Joshua 24:15 (NKJV).
53. Proverbs 4:23 (*Jubilee Bible*, 2000).
54. Mathew 20:24-28 (AMP).
55. Romans 12:21 (AMP).
56. Acts 20:35 (AMP).
57. Mathew 6:33 (NKJV).
58. Mathew 10:39 (NKJV).
59. Galatians 5:22 (NKJV).
60. Psalms 111:7; Jeremiah 10:10 (AMP).
61. John 8:44 (AMP).
62. Psalms 116:10 (AMP).
63. Proverbs 18:21 (NKJV).
64. 2 Corinthians 6:7 (EXP).
65. 1 Samuel 17:26b (NKJV).
66. http://en.wikipedia.org/wiki/Nothing_to_fear_but_fear_itself
67. 2 Timothy 1:7 (NKJV).
68. Galatians 1:4; Ephesians 1:20-33 (AMP).
69. Isaiah 55:11 (AMP).
70. Mark 9:17-18 (AMP).
71. Mark 9:24 (NKJV).
72. Cecil Murphy, *Gifted Hands: The Ben Carson Story* (Grand Rapids: Zondervan Publishing House, 2006), 224.
73. *Braveheart*, Paramount Pictures, 1995, 177 minutes.
74. Psalms 91:1 (AMP).
75. Luke 23:34 (*Complete Jewish Bible*).

76. Acts 7:60 (Phillips).
77. Matthew 6:10 (EXB).
78. Luke 17:21 (NKJV).
79. Deuteronomy 11:24 (NKJV).
80. Isaiah 40:31 (NKJV).
81. William Shakespeare, *Hamlet*, act 1, scene 3, 75.
82. Deuteronomy 30:19 (MSG).
83. Psalms 111:10 (NKJV).
84. http://thinkexist.com/quotations/time. Commencement address, Stanford University, June 12, 2005.
85. Proverbs 17:22 (NIV).
86. Ecclesiastes 3:4 (NIV).
87. Psalms 91:1-3 (MSG).
88. Matthew 9:11 (MSG).
89. Luke 7:34 (NIV).
90. James 4:10 (NKJV).
91. Ephesians 4:26 (NKJV).
92. Galatians 6:2 (EXB).
93. Colossians 3:13 (AMP), 1 Peter 4:8 (Easy-to-Read Version).
94. Colossians 3:14 (NKJV).
95. 2 Corinthians 12:9 (NLT).
96. Jane Hansen, *The Journey of a Woman* (Ventura: Gospel Light Publications, 1998), 139.
97. Acts 20:1-2 (MSG).
98. Genesis 2:18 (NKJV).
99. John 8:32 (NIV).
100. *Pay it Forward*, Warner Bros., 2001, DVD.
101. Kevin Dedmon & Chad Dedmon, *Risk Factor* (Shippensburg: Destiny Image Publishers, Inc., 2011), 1-205.
102. http://www.inspirational-quotes-and-quotations.com/inspiring-quote-by-thomas-edison.html.
103. Genesis 2:7 (AMP).
104. Genesis 1:27 (MSG).

105. Peoplesworld.org.
106. Matthew 26: 69-75 (NKJV).
107. The Holy Bible, Book of Exodus.
108. *Iron Will* (Walt Disney Pictures, 1994).
109. *We Are Marshall* (Warner Bros., 2006).
110. *Lord of the Rings: The Fellowship of the Ring* (New Line Cinema, 2001).
111. *Star Trek* (Paramount Pictures, 2009).
112. *Iron Will.*
113. *We Are Marshall.*
114. *Lord of the Rings: The Fellowship of the Ring.*
115. *Star Trek.*

ABOUT JULIE

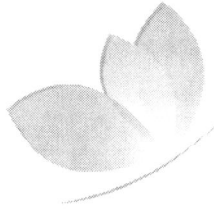

New Life for Today was founded by Julie Court in 2009 to rescue the lost, heal the sick, and free the captive. Julie's anointed teaching simplifies complex biblical truths to guide you into a closer relationship with Father God, Jesus, and Holy Spirit. By learning to obey the Holy Spirit, you will grow spiritually, discover your God-given gifts, and be equipped for ministry.

Julie aggressively pursues the dreams God has for her. Her intimate connection to God, even amidst painful life experiences, inspires others to seek face-to-face encounters with the King of Kings. She seeks out the ways, purposes, and mysteries of her Father and shares them to equip the body of Christ to make their supply in expanding the Kingdom.

Julie is a former business owner, ghostwriter for articles on wellness, speaker and educator, planner and organizer for international missions trips, and has experience in many other areas of both corporate and community organizations. She currently speaks to church and community groups, hosts conferences, and runs her non-profit ministry, New Life for Today.

Julie has traveled internationally and in the Midwest as a prophetic Bible teacher. God has called her to travel to ten countries and four continents to share the message of the kingdom. In third-world countries, New Life for Today sponsors pastors and women's conferences, crusades, and humanitarian relief. She was commissioned into the ministry in Israel in 2008.

Julie speaks and teaches on a variety of subjects. To schedule an interview, a speaking engagement, or a one-day, interactive *Incredible Life Makeover* Workshop, please check out her resources at **Newlifefortoday.com**.

You can follow Julie on Facebook, Twitter, and her weekly blog as she endeavors to help others find the path to freedom. You can contact Julie at newlife4today@gmail.com.

CONTACT INFORMATION

REDEMPTION
PRESS

To order additional copies of this book,
please visit www.newlifefortoday.com
or
www.redemption-press.com.
Also available on Amazon.com and BarnesandNoble.com
Or by calling toll free 1-844-2REDEEM.

CPSIA information can be obtained
at www.ICGtesting.com
Printed in the USA
FFOW01n1831250618
47247444-50109FF